D1737404

THIS IS YOUR **PASSBOOK®** FOR ...

OFFICE TECHNICIAN

NATIONAL LEARNING CORPORATION®

passbooks.com

Copyright © 2018 by

National Learning Corporation

212 Michael Drive, Syosset, NY 11791
(516) 921-8888 • www.passbooks.com
E-mail: info@passbooks.com

PUBLISHED IN THE UNITED STATES OF AMERICA

PASSBOOK® SERIES

THE *PASSBOOK® SERIES* has been created to prepare applicants and candidates for the ultimate academic battlefield – the examination room.

At some time in our lives, each and every one of us may be required to take an examination – for validation, matriculation, admission, qualification, registration, certification, or licensure.

Based on the assumption that every applicant or candidate has met the basic formal educational standards, has taken the required number of courses, and read the necessary texts, the *PASSBOOK® SERIES* furnishes the one special preparation which may assure passing with confidence, instead of failing with insecurity. Examination questions – together with answers – are furnished as the basic vehicle for study so that the mysteries of the examination and its compounding difficulties may be eliminated or diminished by a sure method.

This book is meant to help you pass your examination provided that you qualify and are serious in your objective.

The entire field is reviewed through the huge store of content information which is succinctly presented through a provocative and challenging approach – the question-and-answer method.

A climate of success is established by furnishing the correct answers at the end of each test.

You soon learn to recognize types of questions, forms of questions, and patterns of questioning. You may even begin to anticipate expected outcomes.

You perceive that many questions are repeated or adapted so that you can gain acute insights, which may enable you to score many sure points.

You learn how to confront new questions, or types of questions, and to attack them confidently and work out the correct answers.

You note objectives and emphases, and recognize pitfalls and dangers, so that you may make positive educational adjustments.

Moreover, you are kept fully informed in relation to new concepts, methods, practices, and directions in the field.

You discover that you arre actually taking the examination all the time: you are preparing for the examination by "taking" an examination, not by reading extraneous and/or supererogatory textbooks.

In short, this PASSBOOK®, used directedly, should be an important factor in helping you to pass your test.

OFFICE TECHNICIAN

DUTIES:
This is the advanced journey level which regularly performs a variety of the most difficult duties and is expected to consistently exercise a high degree of initiative, independence and originality in performing assigned tasks. Positions at this level regularly require detailed and sensitive public contact and/or independent correspondence involving the knowledge and application of detailed regulations, policies and procedures. Good judgment and the ability to communicate effectively are of primary importance at this level. Typically, the work at this level is rarely reviewed. In addition, positions may have responsibility for functional guidance in training and assisting less experienced employees.

KNOWLEDGE OF:
- Modern office methods, supplies and equipment.
- Business English and correspondence.
- Principles of effective training.

ABILITY TO:
- Perform difficult clerical work, including ability to spell correctly.
- Use good English.
- Make arithmetical computations.
- Follow oral and written directions.
- Evaluate situations accurately and take effective action.
- Read and write English at a level required for successful job performance.
- Make clear and comprehensive reports and keep difficult records.
- Meet and deal tactfully with the public.
- Apply specific laws, rules and office policies and procedures.
- Prepare correspondence independently utilizing a wide knowledge of vocabulary, grammar and spelling.
- Communicate effectively.
- Provide functional guidance.

SCOPE OF THE EXAMINATION
The written test will be designed to test for knowledge, skills, and/or abilities in such areas as:
1. Arithmetical computation;
2. Communication, including effective english expression;
3. Reading Comprehension;
4. Clerical and verbal abilities, including vocabulary, grammar and spelling;
5. Following oral and written directions; and
6. Office situations.

HOW TO TAKE A TEST

I. YOU MUST PASS AN EXAMINATION

A. *WHAT EVERY CANDIDATE SHOULD KNOW*

Examination applicants often ask us for help in preparing for the written test. What can I study in advance? What kinds of questions will be asked? How will the test be given? How will the papers be graded?

As an applicant for a civil service examination, you may be wondering about some of these things. Our purpose here is to suggest effective methods of advance study and to describe civil service examinations.

Your chances for success on this examination can be increased if you know how to prepare. Those "pre-examination jitters" can be reduced if you know what to expect. You can even experience an adventure in good citizenship if you know why civil service exams are given.

B. *WHY ARE CIVIL SERVICE EXAMINATIONS GIVEN?*

Civil service examinations are important to you in two ways. As a citizen, you want public jobs filled by employees who know how to do their work. As a job seeker, you want a fair chance to compete for that job on an equal footing with other candidates. The best-known means of accomplishing this two-fold goal is the competitive examination.

Exams are widely publicized throughout the nation. They may be administered for jobs in federal, state, city, municipal, town or village governments or agencies.

Any citizen may apply, with some limitations, such as the age or residence of applicants. Your experience and education may be reviewed to see whether you meet the requirements for the particular examination. When these requirements exist, they are reasonable and applied consistently to all applicants. Thus, a competitive examination may cause you some uneasiness now, but it is your privilege and safeguard.

C. *HOW ARE CIVIL SERVICE EXAMS DEVELOPED?*

Examinations are carefully written by trained technicians who are specialists in the field known as "psychological measurement," in consultation with recognized authorities in the field of work that the test will cover. These experts recommend the subject matter areas or skills to be tested; only those knowledges or skills important to your success on the job are included. The most reliable books and source materials available are used as references. Together, the experts and technicians judge the difficulty level of the questions.

Test technicians know how to phrase questions so that the problem is clearly stated. Their ethics do not permit "trick" or "catch" questions. Questions may have been tried out on sample groups, or subjected to statistical analysis, to determine their usefulness.

Written tests are often used in combination with performance tests, ratings of training and experience, and oral interviews. All of these measures combine to form the best-known means of finding the right person for the right job.

II. HOW TO PASS THE WRITTEN TEST

A. NATURE OF THE EXAMINATION

To prepare intelligently for civil service examinations, you should know how they differ from school examinations you have taken. In school you were assigned certain definite pages to read or subjects to cover. The examination questions were quite detailed and usually emphasized memory. Civil service exams, on the other hand, try to discover your present ability to perform the duties of a position, plus your potentiality to learn these duties. In other words, a civil service exam attempts to predict how successful you will be. Questions cover such a broad area that they cannot be as minute and detailed as school exam questions.

In the public service similar kinds of work, or positions, are grouped together in one "class." This process is known as *position-classification*. All the positions in a class are paid according to the salary range for that class. One class title covers all of these positions, and they are all tested by the same examination.

B. FOUR BASIC STEPS

1) Study the announcement

How, then, can you know what subjects to study? Our best answer is: "Learn as much as possible about the class of positions for which you've applied." The exam will test the knowledge, skills and abilities needed to do the work.

Your most valuable source of information about the position you want is the official exam announcement. This announcement lists the training and experience qualifications. Check these standards and apply only if you come reasonably close to meeting them.

The brief description of the position in the examination announcement offers some clues to the subjects which will be tested. Think about the job itself. Review the duties in your mind. Can you perform them, or are there some in which you are rusty? Fill in the blank spots in your preparation.

Many jurisdictions preview the written test in the exam announcement by including a section called "Knowledge and Abilities Required," "Scope of the Examination," or some similar heading. Here you will find out specifically what fields will be tested.

2) Review your own background

Once you learn in general what the position is all about, and what you need to know to do the work, ask yourself which subjects you already know fairly well and which need improvement. You may wonder whether to concentrate on improving your strong areas or on building some background in your fields of weakness. When the announcement has specified "some knowledge" or "considerable knowledge," or has used adjectives like "beginning principles of…" or "advanced … methods," you can get a clue as to the number and difficulty of questions to be asked in any given field. More questions, and hence broader coverage, would be included for those subjects which are more important in the work. Now weigh your strengths and weaknesses against the job requirements and prepare accordingly.

3) Determine the level of the position

Another way to tell how intensively you should prepare is to understand the level of the job for which you are applying. Is it the entering level? In other words, is this the position in which beginners in a field of work are hired? Or is it an intermediate or advanced level? Sometimes this is indicated by such words as "Junior" or "Senior" in the class title. Other jurisdictions use Roman numerals to designate the level – Clerk I, Clerk II, for example. The word "Supervisor" sometimes appears in the title. If the level is not indicated by the title, check the description of duties. Will you be working under very close supervision, or will you have responsibility for independent decisions in this work?

4) Choose appropriate study materials

Now that you know the subjects to be examined and the relative amount of each subject to be covered, you can choose suitable study materials. For beginning level jobs, or even advanced ones, if you have a pronounced weakness in some aspect of your training, read a modern, standard textbook in that field. Be sure it is up to date and has general coverage. Such books are normally available at your library, and the librarian will be glad to help you locate one. For entry-level positions, questions of appropriate difficulty are chosen – neither highly advanced questions, nor those too simple. Such questions require careful thought but not advanced training.

If the position for which you are applying is technical or advanced, you will read more advanced, specialized material. If you are already familiar with the basic principles of your field, elementary textbooks would waste your time. Concentrate on advanced textbooks and technical periodicals. Think through the concepts and review difficult problems in your field.

These are all general sources. You can get more ideas on your own initiative, following these leads. For example, training manuals and publications of the government agency which employs workers in your field can be useful, particularly for technical and professional positions. A letter or visit to the government department involved may result in more specific study suggestions, and certainly will provide you with a more definite idea of the exact nature of the position you are seeking.

III. KINDS OF TESTS

Tests are used for purposes other than measuring knowledge and ability to perform specified duties. For some positions, it is equally important to test ability to make adjustments to new situations or to profit from training. In others, basic mental abilities not dependent on information are essential. Questions which test these things may not appear as pertinent to the duties of the position as those which test for knowledge and information. Yet they are often highly important parts of a fair examination. For very general questions, it is almost impossible to help you direct your study efforts. What we can do is to point out some of the more common of these general abilities needed in public service positions and describe some typical questions.

1) General information

Broad, general information has been found useful for predicting job success in some kinds of work. This is tested in a variety of ways, from vocabulary lists to questions about current events. Basic background in some field of work, such as sociology or economics, may be sampled in a group of questions. Often these are principles which have become familiar to most persons through exposure rather than through formal training. It is difficult to advise you how to study for these questions; being alert to the world around you is our best suggestion.

2) Verbal ability

An example of an ability needed in many positions is verbal or language ability. Verbal ability is, in brief, the ability to use and understand words. Vocabulary and grammar tests are typical measures of this ability. Reading comprehension or paragraph interpretation questions are common in many kinds of civil service tests. You are given a paragraph of written material and asked to find its central meaning.

3) Numerical ability

Number skills can be tested by the familiar arithmetic problem, by checking paired lists of numbers to see which are alike and which are different, or by interpreting charts and graphs. In the latter test, a graph may be printed in the test booklet which you are asked to use as the basis for answering questions.

4) Observation

A popular test for law-enforcement positions is the observation test. A picture is shown to you for several minutes, then taken away. Questions about the picture test your ability to observe both details and larger elements.

5) Following directions

In many positions in the public service, the employee must be able to carry out written instructions dependably and accurately. You may be given a chart with several columns, each column listing a variety of information. The questions require you to carry out directions involving the information given in the chart.

6) Skills and aptitudes

Performance tests effectively measure some manual skills and aptitudes. When the skill is one in which you are trained, such as typing or shorthand, you can practice. These tests are often very much like those given in business school or high school courses. For many of the other skills and aptitudes, however, no short-time preparation can be made. Skills and abilities natural to you or that you have developed throughout your lifetime are being tested.

Many of the general questions just described provide all the data needed to answer the questions and ask you to use your reasoning ability to find the answers. Your best preparation for these tests, as well as for tests of facts and ideas, is to be at your physical and mental best. You, no doubt, have your own methods of getting into an exam-taking mood and keeping "in shape." The next section lists some ideas on this subject.

IV. KINDS OF QUESTIONS

Only rarely is the "essay" question, which you answer in narrative form, used in civil service tests. Civil service tests are usually of the short-answer type. Full instructions for answering these questions will be given to you at the examination. But in case this is your first experience with short-answer questions and separate answer sheets, here is what you need to know:

1) Multiple-choice Questions

Most popular of the short-answer questions is the "multiple choice" or "best answer" question. It can be used, for example, to test for factual knowledge, ability to solve problems or judgment in meeting situations found at work.

A multiple-choice question is normally one of three types—

- It can begin with an incomplete statement followed by several possible endings. You are to find the one ending which *best* completes the statement, although some of the others may not be entirely wrong.
- It can also be a complete statement in the form of a question which is answered by choosing one of the statements listed.
- It can be in the form of a problem – again you select the best answer.

Here is an example of a multiple-choice question with a discussion which should give you some clues as to the method for choosing the right answer:

When an employee has a complaint about his assignment, the action which will *best* help him overcome his difficulty is to
   A. discuss his difficulty with his coworkers
   B. take the problem to the head of the organization
   C. take the problem to the person who gave him the assignment
   D. say nothing to anyone about his complaint

In answering this question, you should study each of the choices to find which is best. Consider choice "A" – Certainly an employee may discuss his complaint with fellow employees, but no change or improvement can result, and the complaint remains unresolved. Choice "B" is a poor choice since the head of the organization probably does not know what assignment you have been given, and taking your problem to him is known as "going over the head" of the supervisor. The supervisor, or person who made the assignment, is the person who can clarify it or correct any injustice. Choice "C" is, therefore, correct. To say nothing, as in choice "D," is unwise. Supervisors have and interest in knowing the problems employees are facing, and the employee is seeking a solution to his problem.

2) True/False Questions

The "true/false" or "right/wrong" form of question is sometimes used. Here a complete statement is given. Your job is to decide whether the statement is right or wrong.

SAMPLE: A roaming cell-phone call to a nearby city costs less than a non-roaming call to a distant city.

This statement is wrong, or false, since roaming calls are more expensive.

This is not a complete list of all possible question forms, although most of the others are variations of these common types. You will always get complete directions for answering questions. Be sure you understand *how* to mark your answers – ask questions until you do.

V. RECORDING YOUR ANSWERS

Computer terminals are used more and more today for many different kinds of exams.

For an examination with very few applicants, you may be told to record your answers in the test booklet itself. Separate answer sheets are much more common. If this separate answer sheet is to be scored by machine – and this is often the case – it is highly important that you mark your answers correctly in order to get credit.

An electronic scoring machine is often used in civil service offices because of the speed with which papers can be scored. Machine-scored answer sheets must be marked with a pencil, which will be given to you. This pencil has a high graphite content which responds to the electronic scoring machine. As a matter of fact, stray dots may register as answers, so do not let your pencil rest on the answer sheet while you are pondering the correct answer. Also, if your pencil lead breaks or is otherwise defective, ask for another.

Since the answer sheet will be dropped in a slot in the scoring machine, be careful not to bend the corners or get the paper crumpled.

The answer sheet normally has five vertical columns of numbers, with 30 numbers to a column. These numbers correspond to the question numbers in your test booklet. After each number, going across the page are four or five pairs of dotted lines. These short dotted lines have small letters or numbers above them. The first two pairs may also have a "T" or "F" above the letters. This indicates that the first two pairs only are to be used if the questions are of the true-false type. If the questions are multiple choice, disregard the "T" and "F" and pay attention only to the small letters or numbers.

Answer your questions in the manner of the sample that follows:

32. The largest city in the United States is
  A. Washington, D.C.
  B. New York City
  C. Chicago
  D. Detroit
  E. San Francisco

1) Choose the answer you think is best. (New York City is the largest, so "B" is correct.)
2) Find the row of dotted lines numbered the same as the question you are answering. (Find row number 32)
3) Find the pair of dotted lines corresponding to the answer. (Find the pair of lines under the mark "B.")
4) Make a solid black mark between the dotted lines.

VI. BEFORE THE TEST

Common sense will help you find procedures to follow to get ready for an examination. Too many of us, however, overlook these sensible measures. Indeed, nervousness and fatigue have been found to be the most serious reasons why applicants fail to do their best on civil service tests. Here is a list of reminders:

- Begin your preparation early – Don't wait until the last minute to go scurrying around for books and materials or to find out what the position is all about.
- Prepare continuously – An hour a night for a week is better than an all-night cram session. This has been definitely established. What is more, a night a week for a month will return better dividends than crowding your study into a shorter period of time.
- Locate the place of the exam – You have been sent a notice telling you when and where to report for the examination. If the location is in a different town or otherwise unfamiliar to you, it would be well to inquire the best route and learn something about the building.
- Relax the night before the test – Allow your mind to rest. Do not study at all that night. Plan some mild recreation or diversion; then go to bed early and get a good night's sleep.
- Get up early enough to make a leisurely trip to the place for the test – This way unforeseen events, traffic snarls, unfamiliar buildings, etc. will not upset you.
- Dress comfortably – A written test is not a fashion show. You will be known by number and not by name, so wear something comfortable.
- Leave excess paraphernalia at home – Shopping bags and odd bundles will get in your way. You need bring only the items mentioned in the official notice you received; usually everything you need is provided. Do not bring reference books to the exam. They will only confuse those last minutes and be taken away from you when in the test room.
- Arrive somewhat ahead of time – If because of transportation schedules you must get there very early, bring a newspaper or magazine to take your mind off yourself while waiting.
- Locate the examination room – When you have found the proper room, you will be directed to the seat or part of the room where you will sit. Sometimes you are given a sheet of instructions to read while you are waiting. Do not fill out any forms until you are told to do so; just read them and be prepared.
- Relax and prepare to listen to the instructions
- If you have any physical problem that may keep you from doing your best, be sure to tell the test administrator. If you are sick or in poor health, you really cannot do your best on the exam. You can come back and take the test some other time.

VII. AT THE TEST

The day of the test is here and you have the test booklet in your hand. The temptation to get going is very strong. Caution! There is more to success than knowing the right answers. You must know how to identify your papers and understand variations in the type of short-answer question used in this particular examination. Follow these suggestions for maximum results from your efforts:

1) Cooperate with the monitor

The test administrator has a duty to create a situation in which you can be as much at ease as possible. He will give instructions, tell you when to begin, check to see that you are marking your answer sheet correctly, and so on. He is not there to guard you, although he will see that your competitors do not take unfair advantage. He wants to help you do your best.

2) Listen to all instructions

Don't jump the gun! Wait until you understand all directions. In most civil service tests you get more time than you need to answer the questions. So don't be in a hurry. Read each word of instructions until you clearly understand the meaning. Study the examples, listen to all announcements and follow directions. Ask questions if you do not understand what to do.

3) Identify your papers

Civil service exams are usually identified by number only. You will be assigned a number; you must not put your name on your test papers. Be sure to copy your number correctly. Since more than one exam may be given, copy your exact examination title.

4) Plan your time

Unless you are told that a test is a "speed" or "rate of work" test, speed itself is usually not important. Time enough to answer all the questions will be provided, but this does not mean that you have all day. An overall time limit has been set. Divide the total time (in minutes) by the number of questions to determine the approximate time you have for each question.

5) Do not linger over difficult questions

If you come across a difficult question, mark it with a paper clip (useful to have along) and come back to it when you have been through the booklet. One caution if you do this – be sure to skip a number on your answer sheet as well. Check often to be sure that you have not lost your place and that you are marking in the row numbered the same as the question you are answering.

6) Read the questions

Be sure you know what the question asks! Many capable people are unsuccessful because they failed to *read* the questions correctly.

7) Answer all questions

Unless you have been instructed that a penalty will be deducted for incorrect answers, it is better to guess than to omit a question.

8) Speed tests

It is often better NOT to guess on speed tests. It has been found that on timed tests people are tempted to spend the last few seconds before time is called in marking answers at random – without even reading them – in the hope of picking up a few extra points. To discourage this practice, the instructions may warn you that your score will be "corrected" for guessing. That is, a penalty will be applied. The incorrect answers will be deducted from the correct ones, or some other penalty formula will be used.

9) Review your answers

If you finish before time is called, go back to the questions you guessed or omitted to give them further thought. Review other answers if you have time.

10) Return your test materials

If you are ready to leave before others have finished or time is called, take ALL your materials to the monitor and leave quietly. Never take any test material with you. The monitor can discover whose papers are not complete, and taking a test booklet may be grounds for disqualification.

VIII. EXAMINATION TECHNIQUES

1) Read the general instructions carefully. These are usually printed on the first page of the exam booklet. As a rule, these instructions refer to the timing of the examination; the fact that you should not start work until the signal and must stop work at a signal, etc. If there are any *special* instructions, such as a choice of questions to be answered, make sure that you note this instruction carefully.

2) When you are ready to start work on the examination, that is as soon as the signal has been given, read the instructions to each question booklet, underline any key words or phrases, such as *least, best, outline, describe* and the like. In this way you will tend to answer as requested rather than discover on reviewing your paper that you *listed without describing*, that you selected the *worst* choice rather than the *best* choice, etc.

3) If the examination is of the objective or multiple-choice type – that is, each question will also give a series of possible answers: A, B, C or D, and you are called upon to select the best answer and write the letter next to that answer on your answer paper – it is advisable to start answering each question in turn. There may be anywhere from 50 to 100 such questions in the three or four hours allotted and you can see how much time would be taken if you read through all the questions before beginning to answer any. Furthermore, if you come across a question or group of questions which you know would be difficult to answer, it would undoubtedly affect your handling of all the other questions.

4) If the examination is of the essay type and contains but a few questions, it is a moot point as to whether you should read all the questions before starting to answer any one. Of course, if you are given a choice – say five out of seven and the like – then it is essential to read all the questions so you can eliminate the two that are most difficult. If, however, you are asked to answer all the questions, there may be danger in trying to answer the easiest one first because you may find that you will spend too much time on it. The best technique is to answer the first question, then proceed to the second, etc.

5) Time your answers. Before the exam begins, write down the time it started, then add the time allowed for the examination and write down the time it must be completed, then divide the time available somewhat as follows:

- If 3-1/2 hours are allowed, that would be 210 minutes. If you have 80 objective-type questions, that would be an average of 2-1/2 minutes per question. Allow yourself no more than 2 minutes per question, or a total of 160 minutes, which will permit about 50 minutes to review.
- If for the time allotment of 210 minutes there are 7 essay questions to answer, that would average about 30 minutes a question. Give yourself only 25 minutes per question so that you have about 35 minutes to review.

6) The most important instruction is to *read each question* and make sure you know what is wanted. The second most important instruction is to *time yourself properly* so that you answer every question. The third most important instruction is to *answer every question*. Guess if you have to but include something for each question. Remember that you will receive no credit for a blank and will probably receive some credit if you write something in answer to an essay question. If you guess a letter – say "B" for a multiple-choice question – you may have guessed right. If you leave a blank as an answer to a multiple-choice question, the examiners may respect your feelings but it will not add a point to your score. Some exams may penalize you for wrong answers, so in such cases *only*, you may not want to guess unless you have some basis for your answer.

7) Suggestions
   a. Objective-type questions
      1. Examine the question booklet for proper sequence of pages and questions
      2. Read all instructions carefully
      3. Skip any question which seems too difficult; return to it after all other questions have been answered
      4. Apportion your time properly; do not spend too much time on any single question or group of questions
      5. Note and underline key words – *all, most, fewest, least, best, worst, same, opposite,* etc.
      6. Pay particular attention to negatives
      7. Note unusual option, e.g., unduly long, short, complex, different or similar in content to the body of the question
      8. Observe the use of "hedging" words – *probably, may, most likely,* etc.
      9. Make sure that your answer is put next to the same number as the question
      10. Do not second-guess unless you have good reason to believe the second answer is definitely more correct
      11. Cross out original answer if you decide another answer is more accurate; do not erase until you are ready to hand your paper in
      12. Answer all questions; guess unless instructed otherwise
      13. Leave time for review

   b. Essay questions
      1. Read each question carefully
      2. Determine exactly what is wanted. Underline key words or phrases.
      3. Decide on outline or paragraph answer

4. Include many different points and elements unless asked to develop any one or two points or elements
5. Show impartiality by giving pros and cons unless directed to select one side only
6. Make and write down any assumptions you find necessary to answer the questions
7. Watch your English, grammar, punctuation and choice of words
8. Time your answers; don't crowd material

8) Answering the essay question

Most essay questions can be answered by framing the specific response around several key words or ideas. Here are a few such key words or ideas:

M's: manpower, materials, methods, money, management
P's: purpose, program, policy, plan, procedure, practice, problems, pitfalls, personnel, public relations
    a. Six basic steps in handling problems:
        1. Preliminary plan and background development
        2. Collect information, data and facts
        3. Analyze and interpret information, data and facts
        4. Analyze and develop solutions as well as make recommendations
        5. Prepare report and sell recommendations
        6. Install recommendations and follow up effectiveness

    b. Pitfalls to avoid
        1. *Taking things for granted* – A statement of the situation does not necessarily imply that each of the elements is necessarily true; for example, a complaint may be invalid and biased so that all that can be taken for granted is that a complaint has been registered
        2. *Considering only one side of a situation* – Wherever possible, indicate several alternatives and then point out the reasons you selected the best one
        3. *Failing to indicate follow up* – Whenever your answer indicates action on your part, make certain that you will take proper follow-up action to see how successful your recommendations, procedures or actions turn out to be
        4. *Taking too long in answering any single question* – Remember to time your answers properly

IX. AFTER THE TEST

Scoring procedures differ in detail among civil service jurisdictions although the general principles are the same. Whether the papers are hand-scored or graded by machine we have described, they are nearly always graded by number. That is, the person who marks the paper knows only the number – never the name – of the applicant. Not until all the papers have been graded will they be matched with names. If other tests, such as training and experience or oral interview ratings have been given, scores will be combined. Different parts of the examination usually have different weights. For example, the written test might count 60 percent of the final grade, and a rating of training and experience 40 percent. In many jurisdictions, veterans will have a certain number of points added to their grades.

After the final grade has been determined, the names are placed in grade order and an eligible list is established. There are various methods for resolving ties between those who get the same final grade – probably the most common is to place first the name of the person whose application was received first. Job offers are made from the eligible list in the order the names appear on it. You will be notified of your grade and your rank as soon as all these computations have been made. This will be done as rapidly as possible.

People who are found to meet the requirements in the announcement are called "eligibles." Their names are put on a list of eligible candidates. An eligible's chances of getting a job depend on how high he stands on this list and how fast agencies are filling jobs from the list.

When a job is to be filled from a list of eligibles, the agency asks for the names of people on the list of eligibles for that job. When the civil service commission receives this request, it sends to the agency the names of the three people highest on this list. Or, if the job to be filled has specialized requirements, the office sends the agency the names of the top three persons who meet these requirements from the general list.

The appointing officer makes a choice from among the three people whose names were sent to him. If the selected person accepts the appointment, the names of the others are put back on the list to be considered for future openings.

That is the rule in hiring from all kinds of eligible lists, whether they are for typist, carpenter, chemist, or something else. For every vacancy, the appointing officer has his choice of any one of the top three eligibles on the list. This explains why the person whose name is on top of the list sometimes does not get an appointment when some of the persons lower on the list do. If the appointing officer chooses the second or third eligible, the No. 1 eligible does not get a job at once, but stays on the list until he is appointed or the list is terminated.

X. HOW TO PASS THE INTERVIEW TEST

The examination for which you applied requires an oral interview test. You have already taken the written test and you are now being called for the interview test – the final part of the formal examination.

You may think that it is not possible to prepare for an interview test and that there are no procedures to follow during an interview. Our purpose is to point out some things you can do in advance that will help you and some good rules to follow and pitfalls to avoid while you are being interviewed.

What is an interview supposed to test?

The written examination is designed to test the technical knowledge and competence of the candidate; the oral is designed to evaluate intangible qualities, not readily measured otherwise, and to establish a list showing the relative fitness of each candidate – as measured against his competitors – for the position sought. Scoring is not on the basis of "right" and "wrong," but on a sliding scale of values ranging from "not passable" to "outstanding." As a matter of fact, it is possible to achieve a relatively low score without a single "incorrect" answer because of evident weakness in the qualities being measured.

Occasionally, an examination may consist entirely of an oral test – either an individual or a group oral. In such cases, information is sought concerning the technical knowledges and abilities of the candidate, since there has been no written examination for this purpose. More commonly, however, an oral test is used to supplement a written examination.

Who conducts interviews?

The composition of oral boards varies among different jurisdictions. In nearly all, a representative of the personnel department serves as chairman. One of the members of the board may be a representative of the department in which the candidate would work. In some cases, "outside experts" are used, and, frequently, a businessman or some other representative of the general public is asked to serve. Labor and management or other special groups may be represented. The aim is to secure the services of experts in the appropriate field.

However the board is composed, it is a good idea (and not at all improper or unethical) to ascertain in advance of the interview who the members are and what groups they represent. When you are introduced to them, you will have some idea of their backgrounds and interests, and at least you will not stutter and stammer over their names.

What should be done before the interview?

While knowledge about the board members is useful and takes some of the surprise element out of the interview, there is other preparation which is more substantive. It *is* possible to prepare for an oral interview – in several ways:

1) Keep a copy of your application and review it carefully before the interview

This may be the only document before the oral board, and the starting point of the interview. Know what education and experience you have listed there, and the sequence and dates of all of it. Sometimes the board will ask you to review the highlights of your experience for them; you should not have to hem and haw doing it.

2) Study the class specification and the examination announcement

Usually, the oral board has one or both of these to guide them. The qualities, characteristics or knowledges required by the position sought are stated in these documents. They offer valuable clues as to the nature of the oral interview. For example, if the job involves supervisory responsibilities, the announcement will usually indicate that knowledge of modern supervisory methods and the qualifications of the candidate as a supervisor will be tested. If so, you can expect such questions, frequently in the form of a hypothetical situation which you are expected to solve. NEVER go into an oral without knowledge of the duties and responsibilities of the job you seek.

3) Think through each qualification required

Try to visualize the kind of questions you would ask if you were a board member. How well could you answer them? Try especially to appraise your own knowledge and background in each area, *measured against the job sought*, and identify any areas in which you are weak. Be critical and realistic – do not flatter yourself.

4) Do some general reading in areas in which you feel you may be weak

For example, if the job involves supervision and your past experience has NOT, some general reading in supervisory methods and practices, particularly in the field of human relations, might be useful. Do NOT study agency procedures or detailed manuals. The oral board will be testing your understanding and capacity, not your memory.

5) Get a good night's sleep and watch your general health and mental attitude

You will want a clear head at the interview. Take care of a cold or any other minor ailment, and of course, no hangovers.

What should be done on the day of the interview?

Now comes the day of the interview itself. Give yourself plenty of time to get there. Plan to arrive somewhat ahead of the scheduled time, particularly if your appointment is in the fore part of the day. If a previous candidate fails to appear, the board might be ready for you a bit early. By early afternoon an oral board is almost invariably behind schedule if there are many candidates, and you may have to wait. Take along a book or magazine to read, or your application to review, but leave any extraneous material in the waiting room when you go in for your interview. In any event, relax and compose yourself.

The matter of dress is important. The board is forming impressions about you – from your experience, your manners, your attitude, and your appearance. Give your personal appearance careful attention. Dress your best, but not your flashiest. Choose conservative, appropriate clothing, and be sure it is immaculate. This is a business interview, and your appearance should indicate that you regard it as such. Besides, being well groomed and properly dressed will help boost your confidence.

Sooner or later, someone will call your name and escort you into the interview room. *This is it.* From here on you are on your own. It is too late for any more preparation. But remember, you asked for this opportunity to prove your fitness, and you are here because your request was granted.

What happens when you go in?

The usual sequence of events will be as follows: The clerk (who is often the board stenographer) will introduce you to the chairman of the oral board, who will introduce you to the other members of the board. Acknowledge the introductions before you sit down. Do not be surprised if you find a microphone facing you or a stenotypist sitting by. Oral interviews are usually recorded in the event of an appeal or other review.

Usually the chairman of the board will open the interview by reviewing the highlights of your education and work experience from your application – primarily for the benefit of the other members of the board, as well as to get the material into the record. Do not interrupt or comment unless there is an error or significant misinterpretation; if that is the case, do not hesitate. But do not quibble about insignificant matters. Also, he will usually ask you some question about your education, experience or your present job – partly to get you to start talking and to establish the interviewing "rapport." He may start the actual questioning, or turn it over to one of the other members. Frequently, each member undertakes the questioning on a particular area, one in which he is perhaps most competent, so you can expect each member to participate in the examination. Because time is limited, you may also expect some rather abrupt switches in the direction the questioning takes, so do not be upset by it. Normally, a board member will not pursue a single line of questioning unless he discovers a particular strength or weakness.

After each member has participated, the chairman will usually ask whether any member has any further questions, then will ask you if you have anything you wish to add. Unless you are expecting this question, it may floor you. Worse, it may start you off on an extended, extemporaneous speech. The board is not usually seeking more information. The question is principally to offer you a last opportunity to present further qualifications or to indicate that you have nothing to add. So, if you feel that a significant qualification or characteristic has been overlooked, it is proper to point it out in a sentence or so. Do not compliment the board on the thoroughness of their examination – they have been sketchy, and you know it. If you wish, merely say, "No thank you, I have nothing further to add." This is a point where you can "talk yourself out" of a good impression or fail to present an important bit of information. Remember, *you close the interview yourself.*

The chairman will then say, "That is all, Mr. _____, thank you." Do not be startled; the interview is over, and quicker than you think. Thank him, gather your belongings and take your leave. Save your sigh of relief for the other side of the door.

How to put your best foot forward

Throughout this entire process, you may feel that the board individually and collectively is trying to pierce your defenses, seek out your hidden weaknesses and embarrass and confuse you. Actually, this is not true. They are obliged to make an appraisal of your qualifications for the job you are seeking, and they want to see you in your best light. Remember, they must interview all candidates and a non-cooperative candidate may become a failure in spite of their best efforts to bring out his qualifications. Here are 15 suggestions that will help you:

1) Be natural – Keep your attitude confident, not cocky

If you are not confident that you can do the job, do not expect the board to be. Do not apologize for your weaknesses, try to bring out your strong points. The board is interested in a positive, not negative, presentation. Cockiness will antagonize any board member and make him wonder if you are covering up a weakness by a false show of strength.

2) Get comfortable, but don't lounge or sprawl

Sit erectly but not stiffly. A careless posture may lead the board to conclude that you are careless in other things, or at least that you are not impressed by the importance of the occasion. Either conclusion is natural, even if incorrect. Do not fuss with your clothing, a pencil or an ashtray. Your hands may occasionally be useful to emphasize a point; do not let them become a point of distraction.

3) Do not wisecrack or make small talk

This is a serious situation, and your attitude should show that you consider it as such. Further, the time of the board is limited – they do not want to waste it, and neither should you.

4) Do not exaggerate your experience or abilities

In the first place, from information in the application or other interviews and sources, the board may know more about you than you think. Secondly, you probably will not get away with it. An experienced board is rather adept at spotting such a situation, so do not take the chance.

5) If you know a board member, do not make a point of it, yet do not hide it

Certainly you are not fooling him, and probably not the other members of the board. Do not try to take advantage of your acquaintanceship – it will probably do you little good.

6) Do not dominate the interview

Let the board do that. They will give you the clues – do not assume that you have to do all the talking. Realize that the board has a number of questions to ask you, and do not try to take up all the interview time by showing off your extensive knowledge of the answer to the first one.

7) Be attentive

You only have 20 minutes or so, and you should keep your attention at its sharpest throughout. When a member is addressing a problem or question to you, give him your undivided attention. Address your reply principally to him, but do not exclude the other board members.

8) Do not interrupt

A board member may be stating a problem for you to analyze. He will ask you a question when the time comes. Let him state the problem, and wait for the question.

9) Make sure you understand the question

Do not try to answer until you are sure what the question is. If it is not clear, restate it in your own words or ask the board member to clarify it for you. However, do not haggle about minor elements.

10) Reply promptly but not hastily

A common entry on oral board rating sheets is "candidate responded readily," or "candidate hesitated in replies." Respond as promptly and quickly as you can, but do not jump to a hasty, ill-considered answer.

11) Do not be peremptory in your answers

A brief answer is proper – but do not fire your answer back. That is a losing game from your point of view. The board member can probably ask questions much faster than you can answer them.

12) Do not try to create the answer you think the board member wants

He is interested in what kind of mind you have and how it works – not in playing games. Furthermore, he can usually spot this practice and will actually grade you down on it.

13) Do not switch sides in your reply merely to agree with a board member

Frequently, a member will take a contrary position merely to draw you out and to see if you are willing and able to defend your point of view. Do not start a debate, yet do not surrender a good position. If a position is worth taking, it is worth defending.

14) Do not be afraid to admit an error in judgment if you are shown to be wrong

      The board knows that you are forced to reply without any opportunity for careful consideration. Your answer may be demonstrably wrong. If so, admit it and get on with the interview.

15) Do not dwell at length on your present job

      The opening question may relate to your present assignment. Answer the question but do not go into an extended discussion. You are being examined for a *new* job, not your present one. As a matter of fact, try to phrase ALL your answers in terms of the job for which you are being examined.

Basis of Rating

      Probably you will forget most of these "do's" and "don'ts" when you walk into the oral interview room. Even remembering them all will not ensure you a passing grade. Perhaps you did not have the qualifications in the first place. But remembering them will help you to put your best foot forward, without treading on the toes of the board members.

      Rumor and popular opinion to the contrary notwithstanding, an oral board wants you to make the best appearance possible. They know you are under pressure – but they also want to see how you respond to it as a guide to what your reaction would be under the pressures of the job you seek. They will be influenced by the degree of poise you display, the personal traits you show and the manner in which you respond.

ABOUT THIS BOOK

      This book contains tests divided into Examination Sections. Go through each test, answering every question in the margin. At the end of each test look at the answer key and check your answers. On the ones you got wrong, look at the right answer choice and learn. Do not fill in the answers first. Do not memorize the questions and answers, but understand the answer and principles involved. On your test, the questions will likely be different from the samples. Questions are changed and new ones added. If you understand these past questions you should have success with any changes that arise. Tests may consist of several types of questions. We have additional books on each subject should more study be advisable or necessary for you. Finally, the more you study, the better prepared you will be. This book is intended to be the last thing you study before you walk into the examination room. Prior study of relevant texts is also recommended. NLC publishes some of these in our Fundamental Series. Knowledge and good sense are important factors in passing your exam. Good luck also helps. So now study this Passbook, absorb the material contained within and take that knowledge into the examination. Then do your best to pass that exam.

———

EXAMINATION SECTION

EXAMINATION SECTION
TEST 1

DIRECTIONS: Each question or incomplete statement is followed by several suggested answers or completions. Select the one that BEST answers the question or completes the statement. *PRINT THE LETTER OF THE CORRECT ANSWER IN THE SPACE AT THE RIGHT.*

Questions 1 through 3 refer to the following passage:

When you look at a large factory, you probably do not think about the trees growing in the park. But green plants are a special kind of factory all their own. Using nothing more than water and sunlight, green plants have the unique ability to produce their own food. At the same time, they also make it possible for other living things to exist.

All of this work is done by their leaves. Special cells in the leaves absorb energy from sunlight. This light energy reacts with water that the plant has absorbed from the ground and splits the water into two chemicals. One chemical, oxygen, is released into the air. The other chemical, hydrogen, helps produce sugars that enable the plant to grow new stems, leaves, blossoms and seeds.

By making their own food, plants accomplish several things. They keep themselves alive. They grow the seeds needed to reproduce. They produce the pollen that enables other plants of their kind to reproduce. Meanwhile, the oxygen released into the air makes it possible for other living things to survive.

Human beings have created factories that make wonderful products for us to use and enjoy. But the "living factories" that nature has created produce something even more speciallife.

1. Read the sentence below, taken from the first paragraph of the passage: 1.____

   Using nothing more than water and sunlight, green plants have the <u>unique</u> ability to produce their own food.

   Select the word that has the *opposite* meaning of the word <u>unique</u> as it is used in the sentence above.

   A. interesting
   B. distinctive
   C. common
   D. unusual

2. Which sentence best expresses the main idea of the passage?   2.____

   A. Most of the living things on Earth depend upon green plants
   B. Green plants are a very special kind of living factory
   C. Leaves do the most important work for green plants
   D. Human factories and nature's factories have a lot in common

1

3. According to the passage, what happens first when sunlight falls on plant leaves? 3.___

    A.   The plant produces new stems, leaves and blossoms
    •B.   Special cells in the leaves absorb energy in the sun's rays
    C.   Sugars in the leaves are released that feed the plant
    D.   The leaves absorb water from the ground

4. The pie chart below shows the monthly expenses for a company. Which of the following 4.___
is the best approximation of the percentage of expenses spent on raw materials?

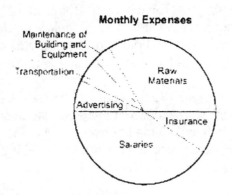

    A. 15%   B. 25%   C. 33%   D. 66%

5. In which sentence is the *correct* verb form used? 5.___

    A.   Mathematics continue to be a difficult subject for many high school students
    B.   All of the runners is expected to do well in the race
    C.   Which of the seniors have been selected as class president?
    D.   The film consists primarily of interviews with world-famous scientists

6. Which sentence is constructed *correctly*? 6.___

    A.   All of the students in the class did his part to make the play a big success
    B.   Ms. Jones is one of those teachers who are always trying to make her classes more interesting
    C.   Last year, Ms. Jones encouraged the students in her drama class to produce one-act plays
    D.   Ms. Jones hopes the auditorium will have their own stage lights next year

7. Which sentence is punctuated *incorrectly*? 7.___

    A.   According to the curriculum guidelines, students need to learn about the working world.
    B.   Working with local businesses is valuable; it provides an interesting and rewarding experience.
    C.   Farmers and merchants, as well as health workers, are involved in the program.
    D.   Students get actual working experience; while also attending classes.

8. Which underlined word in the sentence below is spelled *correctly*? 8.___
The <u>realisation</u> that they were facing an outbreak of typhoid was an <u>ominnous</u> development with potentially <u>ghastly consaquences</u>.

    A. realisation   B. ominnous   C. ghastly   D. consaquences

9. 0.07 is equal to

    A. 7/100
    B. 1/7
    C. 7/10
    D. 10/7

9.____

10. Select the number that is missing in the problem below:
1,806 - = 358

    A. 1,448
    B. 1,756
    C. 2,164
    D. 2,774

10.____

11. Which number is a multiple of 7?

    A. 27   B. 48   C. 52   D. 63

11.____

12. What is 4% of 400?

    A. 16   B. 64   C. 100   D. 160

12.____

_____

KEY (CORRECT ANSWERS)

1.	C		7.	D
2.	B		8.	C
3.	B		9.	A
4.	C		10.	A
5.	D		11.	D
6.	C		12.	A

_____

EXAMINATION SECTION
TEST 1

DIRECTIONS: Each question or incomplete statement is followed by several suggested answers or completions. Select the one that *BEST* answers the question or completes the statement. *PRINT THE LETTER OF THE CORRECT ANSWER IN THE SPACE AT THE RIGHT.*

Questions 1-5.

DIRECTIONS: Each question from 1 to 5 consists of a sentence with an underlined word. For each question, select the choice that is *CLOSEST* in meaning to the underlined word.

EXAMPLE
This division reviews the <u>fiscal</u> reports of the agency.
In this sentence the word *fiscal* means most nearly
A.   financial   B.   critical   C.   basic   D.   personnel
The correct answer is A. "financial" because "financial"
is closest to *fiscal*. Therefore, the answer is A.

1.   Every good office worker needs <u>basic</u> skills.
     The word *basic* in this sentence means   1._____

     A.   fundamental   B.   advanced   C.   unusual   D.   outstanding

2.   He turned out to be a good <u>instructor</u>.   2._____
     The word *instructor* in this sentence means

     A.   student   B.   worker   C.   typist   D.   teacher

3.   The <u>quantity</u> of work in the office was under study.   3._____
     In this sentence, the word *quantity* means

     A.   amount   B.   flow   C.   supervision   D.   type

4.   The morning was spent <u>examining</u> the time records.   4._____
     In this sentence, the word *examining* means

     A.   distributing   B.   collecting   C.   checking   D.   filing

5.   The candidate filled in the <u>proper</u> spaces on the form.   5._____
     In this sentence, the word *proper* means

     A.   blank   B.   appropriate   C.   many   D.   remaining

Questions 6-8.

DIRECTIONS: You are to answer Questions 6 through 8 *SOLELY* on the basis of the information contained in the following paragraph:
     The increase in the number of public documents in the last two centuries closely matches the increase in population in the United States. The great number of public documents has become a serious threat to their usefulness. It is necessary to have programs which will reduce the number of public documents that are kept and which will, at the same time, assure keeping those that have value. Such programs need a great deal of thought to have any success.

6. According to the above paragraph, public documents may be less useful if   6.____

    A. the files are open to the public
    B. the record room is too small
    C. the copying machine is operated only during normal working hours
    D. too many records are being kept

7. According to the above paragraph, the growth of the population in the United States has   7.____
matched the growth in the quantity of public documents for a period of, most nearly,

    A. 50 years   B. 100 years   C. 200 years   D. 300 years

8. According to the above paragraph, the increased number of public documents has made   8.____
it necessary to

    A. find out which public documents are worth keeping
    B. reduce the great number of public documents by decreasing government services
    C. eliminate the copying of all original public documents
    D. avoid all new copying devices.

Questions 9-10.

DIRECTIONS: You are to answer Questions 9 and 10 *SOLELY* on the basis of the information
                  contained in the following paragraph:
    The work goals of an agency can best be reached if the employees understand and agree
with these goals. One way to gain such understanding and agreement is for management to
encourage and seriously consider suggestions from employees in the setting of agency goals.

9. On the basis of the paragraph above, the *BEST* way to achieve the work goals of an   9.____
agency is to

    A. make certain that employees work as hard as possible
    B. study the organizational structure of the agency
    C. encourage employees to think seriously about the agency's problems
    D. stimulate employee understanding of the work goals

10. On the basis of the paragraph above, understanding and agreement with agency goals   10.____
can be gained by

    A. allowing the employees to set agency goals
    B. reaching agency goals quickly
    C. legislative review of agency operations
    D. employee participation in setting agency goals

Questions 11-15.

DIRECTIONS: Each of Questions 11 through 15 consists of a group of four words. One word
                  in each group is *INCORRECTLY* spelled. For each question, print the letter of
                  the correct answer in the space at the right that is the same as the letter next
                  to the word which is *INCORRECTLY* spelled.
                                    EXAMPLE
    A. housing   B. certain   C. budgit   D. money

The word "budgit" is incorrectly spelled, because the correct spelling should be "budget." Therefore, the correct answer is C.

11. A. sentince   B. bulletin   C. notice   D. definition   11.____

12. A. appointment   B. exactly   C. typest   D. light   12.____

13. A. penalty   B. suparvise   C. consider   D. division   13.____

14. A. schedule   B. accurate   C. corect   D. simple   14.____

15. A. suggestion   B. installed   C. proper   D. agincy   15.____

Questions 16-20.

DIRECTIONS: Each question from 16 through 20 consists of a sentence which may be
     A. incorrect because of bad word usage, or
     B. incorrect because of bad punctuation, or
     C. incorrect because of bad spelling, or
     D. correct
Read each sentence carefully. Then print in the proper space at the right A, B, C, or D, according to the answer you choose from the four choices listed above. There is only one type of error in each incorrect sentence. If there is no error, the sentence is correct.
EXAMPLE
George Washington was the father of his contry.
This sentence is incorrect because of bad spelling ("contry" instead of "country"). Therefore, the answer is C.

16. The assignment was completed in record time but the payroll for it has not yet been pre-   16. _C_
    parid.

17. The operator, on the other hand, is willing to learn me how to use the mimeograph.   17. _a_

18. She is the prettiest of the three sisters.   18. _d_

19. She doesn't know; if the mail has arrived.   19. _b_

20. The doorknob of the office door is broke.   20. _a_

21. A clerk can process a form in 15 minutes. How many forms can that clerk process in six   21. _c_
    hours?

    A. 10   B. 21   C. 24   D. 90

22. An office staff consists of 120 people. Sixty of them have been assigned to a special   22.____
    project. Of the remaining staff, 20 answer the mail, 10-handle phone calls, and the rest
    operate the office machines. The number of people operating the office machines is

    A. 20   B. 30   C. 40   D. 45

23. An office worker received 65 applications but on the first day had to return 26 of them for   23.____
    being incomplete and on the second day 25 had to be returned for being incomplete.
    How many applications did <u>not</u> have to be returned?

    A. 10   B. 12   C. 14   D. 16

24. An office worker answered 63 phone calls in one day and 91 phone calls the next day. For these 2 days, what was the average number of phone calls he answered per day?

   A. 77   B. 28   C. 82   D. 93

24.____

25. An office worker processed 12 vouchers of $8.75 each, 3 vouchers of $3.68 each, and 2 vouchers of $1.29 each. The total dollar amount of these vouchers is

   A. $116.04   B. $117.52   C. $118.62   D. $119.04

25.____

KEY (CORRECT ANSWERS)

1.	A	11.	A
2.	D	12.	C
3.	A	13.	B
4.	C	14.	C
5.	B	15.	D
6.	D	16.	C
7.	C	17.	A
8.	A	18.	D
9.	D	19.	B
10.	D	20.	A

21.	C
22.	B
23.	C
24.	A
25.	C

TEST 2

DIRECTIONS: Each question or incomplete statement is followed by several suggested answers or completions. Select the one that *BEST* answers the question or completes the statement. *PRINT THE LETTER OF THE CORRECT ANSWER IN THE SPACE AT THE RIGHT.*

Questions 1-5.

DIRECTIONS: Each question from 1 to 5 lists four names. The names may or may not be exactly the same. Compare the names in each question and mark your answer as follows:
Mark your answer A if all the names are different
Mark your answer B if only two names are exactly the same
Mark your answer C if only three names are exactly the same
Mark your answer D if all four names are exactly the same

EXAMPLE
Jensen, Alfred E.
Jensen, Alfred E.
Jensan, Alfred E.
Jensen, Fred E.

Since the name Jensen, Alfred E. appears twice and is exactly the same in both places, the correct answer is B.

1. Riviera, Pedro S.
   Rivers, Pedro S.
   Riviera, Pedro N.
   Riviera, Juan S.

   1.____

2. Guider, Albert
   Guidar, Albert
   Giuder, Alfred
   Guider, Albert

   2.____

3. Blum, Rona
   Blum, Rona
   Blum, Rona
   Blum, Rona

   3.____

4. Raugh, John
   Raugh, James
   Raughe, John
   Raugh, John

   4.____

5. Katz, Stanley
   Katz, Stanley
   Katze, Stanley
   Katz, Stanley

   5.____

Questions 6-10.

DIRECTIONS: Each Question 6 through 10 consists of numbers or letters in Columns I and II. For each question, compare each line of Column I with its corresponding line in Column II and decide how many lines in Column I are *EXACTLY* the same as their corresponding lines in Column II. In your answer space, mark your answer as follows:

Mark your answer A if only *ONE* line in Column I is exactly the same as its corresponding line in Column II
Mark your answer B if only *TWO* lines in Column I are exactly the same as their corresponding lines in Column II
Mark your answer C if only *THREE* lines in Column I are exactly the same as their corresponding lines in Column II
Mark your answer D if all *FOUR* lines in Column I are exactly the same as their corresponding lines in Column II

EXAMPLE

Column I	Column II
1776	1776
1865	1865
1945	1945
1976	1978

Only three lines in Column I are exactly the same as their corresponding lines in Column II. Therefore, the correct answer is C.

	Column I	Column II	
6.	5653 8727 ZPSS 4952	5653 8728 ZPSS 9453	6.___
7.	PNJP NJPJ JNPN PNJP	PNPJ NJPJ JNPN PNPJ	7.___
8.	effe uWvw KpGj vmnv	eFfe uWvw KpGg vmnv	8.___
9.	5232 PfrC zssz rwwr	5232 PfrN zzss rwww	9.___
10.	czws cecc thrm lwtz	czws cece thrm lwtz	10.___

Questions 11-15.

DIRECTIONS: Questions 11 through 15 have lines of letters and numbers. Each letter should be matched with its number in accordance with the following table:

Letter	F	R	C	A	W	L	E	N	B	T
Matching Number	0	1	2	3	4	5	6	7	8	9

From the table you can determine that the letter F has the matching number 0 below it, the letter R has the matching number 1 below it, etc.

For each question, compare each line of letters and numbers carefully to see if each letter has its correct matching number. If all the letters and numbers are matched correctly in

none of the lines of the question, mark your answer A
only *one* of the lines of the question, mark your answer B
only *two* of the lines of the question, mark your answer C
all three lines of the question, mark your answer D

EXAMPLE

WBCR   4826
TLBF   9580
ATNE   3986

There is a mistake in the first line because the letter R should have its matching number 1 instead of the number 6.

The second line is correct because each letter shown has the correct matching number.

There is a mistake in the third line because the letter N should have the matching number 7 instead of the number 8,

Since all the letters and numbers are matched correctly in only one of the lines in the sample, the correct answer is B.

11.   EBCT   6829   11._____
           ATWR   3961
           NLBW   7584

12.   RNCT   1729   12._____
           LNCR   5728
           WAEB   5368

13.   NTWB   7948   13._____
           RABL   1385
           TAEF   9360

14.   LWRB   5417   14._____
           RLWN   1647
           CBWA   2843

15.   ABTC   3792   15._____
           WCER   5261
           AWCN   3417

16. Your job often brings you into contact with the public. Of the following, it would be *MOST* desirable to explain the reasons for official actions to people coming into your office for assistance because such explanations   16.____

    A. help build greater understanding between the public and your agency
    B. help build greater self-confidence in city employees
    C. convince the public that nothing they do can upset a city employee
    D. show the public that city employees are intelligent

17. Assume that you strongly dislike one of your co-workers.
You should *FIRST*   17.____

    A. discuss your feeling with the co-worker
    B. demand a transfer to another office
    C. suggest to your supervisor that the co-worker should be observed carefully
    D. try to figure out the reason for this dislike before you say or do anything

18. An office worker who has problems accepting authority is *MOST* likely to find it difficult to   18.____

    A. obey rules   B. understand people
    C. assist other employees   D. follow complex instructions

19. The employees in your office have taken a dislike to one person and frequently annoy her. Your supervisor *should*   19.____

    A. transfer this person to another unit at the first opportunity
    B. try to find out the reason for the staff's attitude before doing anything about it
    C. threaten to transfer the first person observed bothering this person
    D. ignore the situation

20. Assume that your supervisor has asked a worker in your office to get a copy of a report out of the files. You notice the worker has accidentally pulled out the wrong report.
Of the following, the *BEST* way for you to handle this situation is to tell   20.____

    A. the worker about all the difficulties that will result from this error
    B. the worker about her mistake in a nice way
    C. the worker to ignore this error
    D. your supervisor that this worker needs more training in how to use the files

21. Filing systems differ in their efficiency. Which of the following is the *BEST* way to evaluate the efficiency of a filing system?
The   21.____

    A. number of times used per day
    B. amount of material that is received each day for filing
    C. amount of time it takes to locate material
    D. type of locking system used

22. In planning ahead so that a sufficient amount of general office supplies is always available, it would be *LEAST* important to find out the   22.____

    A. current office supply needs of the staff
    B. amount of office supplies used last year
    C. days and times that office supplies can be ordered
    D. agency goals and objectives

23. The *MAIN* reason for establishing routine office work procedures is that once a routine is   23.____
established

    A. work need not be checked for accuracy
    B. all steps in the routine will take an equal amount of time to perform
    C. each time the job is repeated it will take less time to perform
    D. each step in the routine will not have to be planned all over again each time

24. When an office machine centrally located in an agency must be shut down for repairs,   24.____
the bureaus and divisions using this machine should be informed of the

    A. expected length of time before the machine will be in operation again
    B. estimated cost of repairs
    C. efforts being made to avoid future repairs
    D. type of new equipment which the agency may buy in the future to replace the
       machine being repaired

25. If the day's work is properly scheduled, the *MOST* important result would be that the   25.____

    A. supervisor will not have to do much supervision
    B. employee will know what to do next
    C. employee will show greater initiative
    D. job will become routine

KEY (CORRECT ANSWERS)

1.	A		11.	C
2.	B		12.	B
3.	D		13.	D
4.	B		14.	B
5.	C		15.	A
6.	B		16.	A
7.	B		17.	D
8.	B		18.	A
9.	A		19.	B
10.	C		20.	B

21.	C
22.	D
23.	D
24.	A
25.	B

EXAMINATION SECTION
TEST 1

DIRECTIONS: Each question or incomplete statement is followed by several suggested answers or completions. Select the one that BEST answers the question or completes the statement. *PRINT THE LETTER OF THE CORRECT ANSWER IN THE SPACE AT THE RIGHT.*

1. Assume that a few co-workers meet near your desk and talk about personal matters during working hours. Lately, this practice has interfered with your work.
In order to stop this practice, the BEST action for you to take FIRST is to

    A. ask your supervisor to put a stop to the co-workers' meeting near your desk
    B. discontinue any friendship with this group
    C. ask your co-workers not to meet near your desk
    D. request that your desk be moved to another location

1.____

2. In order to maintain office coverage during working hours, your supervisor has scheduled your lunch hour from 1 P.M. to 2 P.M. and your co-worker's lunch hour from 12 P.M. to 1 P.M. Lately, your co-worker has been returning late from lunch each day. As a result, you don't get a full hour since you must return to the office by 2 P.M.
Of the following, the BEST action for you to take FIRST is to

    A. explain to your co-worker in a courteous manner that his lateness is interfering with your right to a full hour for lunch
    B. tell your co-worker that his lateness must stop or you will report him to your supervisor
    C. report your co-worker's lateness to your supervisor
    D. leave at 1 P.M. for lunch, whether your co-worker has returned or not

2.____

3. Assume that, as an office worker, one of your jobs is to open mail sent to your unit, read the mail for content, and send the mail to the appropriate person to handle. You accidentally open and begin to read a letter marked *personal* addressed to a co-worker.
Of the following, the BEST action for you to take is to

    A. report to your supervisor that your co-worker is receiving personal mail at the office
    B. destroy the letter so that your co-worker does not know you saw it
    C. reseal the letter and place it on the co-worker's desk without saying anything
    D. bring the letter to your co-worker and explain that you opened it by accident

3.____

4. Suppose that in evaluating your work, your supervisor gives you an overall good rating, but states that you sometimes turn in work with careless errors.
The BEST action for you to take would be to

    A. ask a co-worker who is good at details to proofread your work
    B. take time to do a careful job, paying more attention to detail
    C. continue working as usual since occasional errors are to be expected
    D. ask your supervisor if she would mind correcting your errors

4.____

5. Assume that you are taking a telephone message for a co-worker who is not in the office at the time.
Of the following, the LEAST important item to write on the message is the

    A. length of the call   B. name of the caller
    C. time of the call   D. telephone number of the caller

5.____

Questions 6-13.

DIRECTIONS: Questions 6 through 13 each consist of a sentence which may or may not be an example of good English. The underlined parts of each sentence may be correct or incorrect. Examine each sentence, considering grammar, punctuation, spelling, and capitalization. If the English usage in the underlined parts of the sentence given is better than any of the changes in the underlined words suggested in Options B, C, or D, choose Option A. If the changes in the underlined words suggested in Options B, C, or D would make the sentence correct, choose the correct option. Do not choose an option that will change the meaning of the sentence.

6. This <u>Fall</u>, the office will be closed on <u>Columbus Day, October</u> 9th.   6.____

    A. Correct as is
    B. fall...Columbus Day, October
    C. Fall...columbus day, October
    D. fall...Columbus Day, october

7. This manual <u>discribes the duties performed</u> by an Office Aide.   7.____

    A. Correct as is
    B. describe the duties performed
    C. discribe the duties performed
    D. describes the duties performed

8. There <u>weren't no</u> paper in the supply closet.   8.____

    A. Correct as is   B. weren't any
    C. wasn't any   D. wasn't no

9. The new employees left <u>there</u> office to attend a meeting.   9.____

    A. Correct as is   B. they're
    C. their   D. thier

10. The office worker started working at <u>8:30 a.m.</u>   10.____

    A. Correct as is   B. 8:30 a.m.
    C. 8;30 a,m.   D. 8:30 am

11. The <u>alphabet, or A to Z sequence</u> are the basis of most filing systems.   11.____

    A. Correct as is
    B. alphabet, or A to Z sequence, is
    C. alphabet, or A to Z sequence are
    D. alphabet, or A too Z sequence, is

12. <u>Those</u> file cabinets are five <u>feet</u> tall.   12.____

    A. Correct as is   B. Them...feet
    C. Those...foot   D. Them...foot

13. The Office Aide checked the <u>register and finding</u> the date of the meeting.　　　　13.____

　　A. Correct as is　　　　　　　　　B. regaster and finding
　　C. register and found　　　　　　　D. regaster and found

Questions 14-21.

DIRECTIONS: Each of Questions 14 through 21 has two lists of numbers. Each list contains three sets of numbers. Check each of the three sets in the list on the right to see if they are the same as the corresponding set in the list on the left. Mark your answers:

　　A. If none of the sets in the right list are the same as those in the left list
　　B. if only one of the sets in the right list are the same as those in the left list
　　C. if only two of the sets in the right list are the same as those in the left list
　　D. if all three sets in the right list are the same as those in the left list

14.　7354183476　　　　　　　　7354983476　　　　　　　14.____
　　4474747744　　　　　　　　4474747774
　　57914302311　　　　　　　　57914302311

15.　7143592185　　　　　　　　7143892185　　　　　　　15.____
　　8344517699　　　　　　　　8344518699
　　9178531263　　　　　　　　9178531263

16.　2572114731　　　　　　　　257214731　　　　　　　　16.____
　　8806835476　　　　　　　　8806835476
　　8255831246　　　　　　　　8255831246

17.　331476853821　　　　　　331476858621　　　　　　17.____
　　6976658532996　　　　　　6976655832996
　　3766042113715　　　　　　3766042113745

18.　8806663315　　　　　　　　8806663315　　　　　　　18.____
　　74477138449　　　　　　　　74477138449
　　211756663666　　　　　　　　211756663666

19.　990006966996　　　　　　99000696996　　　　　　　19.____
　　53022219743　　　　　　　　53022219843
　　4171171117717　　　　　　4171171177717

20.　24400222433004　　　　　24400222433004　　　　　20.____
　　5300030055000355　　　　5300030055500355
　　20000075532002022　　　　20000075532002022

21.　6111666406600001116　　6111666406600011 16　　21.____
　　7111300117001100733　　7111300117001100733
　　26666446664476518　　　26666446664476518

Questions 22-25.

DIRECTIONS: Each of Questions 22 through 25 has two lists of names and addresses. Each list contains three sets of names and addresses. Check each of the three sets in the list on the right to see if they are the same as the corresponding set in the list on the left. Mark your answers:

    A.   if none of the sets in the right list are the same as those in the left list

    B.   if only one of the sets in the right list is the same as those in the left list

    C.   if only two of the sets in the right list are the same as those in the left list

    D.   if all three sets in the right list are the same as those in the left list

22.   Mary T. Berlinger   Mary T. Berlinger   22.____
       2351 Hampton St.   2351 Hampton St.
       Monsey, N.Y. 20117   Monsey, N.Y. 20117

       Eduardo Benes   Eduardo Benes
       473 Kingston Avenue   473 Kingston Avenue
       Central Islip, N.Y. 11734   Central Islip, N.Y. 11734

       Alan Carrington Fuchs   Alan Carrington Fuchs
       17 Gnarled Hollow Road   17 Gnarled Hollow Road
       Los Angeles, CA 91635   Los Angeles, CA 91685

23.   David John Jacobson   David John Jacobson   23.____
       178 35 St. Apt. 4C   178 53 St. Apt. 4C
       New York, N.Y. 00927   New York, N.Y. 00927

       Ann-Marie Calonella   Ann-Marie Calonella
       7243 South Ridge Blvd.   7243 South Ridge Blvd.
       Bakersfield, CA 96714   Bakersfield, CA 96714

       Pauline M. Thompson   Pauline M. Thomson
       872 Linden Ave.   872 Linden Ave.
       Houston, Texas 70321   Houston, Texas 70321

24.   Chester LeRoy Masterton   Chester LeRoy Masterson   24.____
       152 Lacy Rd.   152 Lacy Rd.
       Kankakee, Ill. 54532   Kankakee, Ill. 54532

       William Maloney   William Maloney
       S. LaCrosse Pla.   S. LaCross Pla.
       Wausau, Wisconsin 52146   Wausau, Wisconsin 52146

       Cynthia V. Barnes   Cynthia V. Barnes
       16 Pines Rd.   16 Pines Rd.
       Greenpoint, Miss. 20376   Greenpoint, Miss. 20376

25. Marcel Jean Frontenac
6 Burton On The Water
Calender, Me. 01471

Marcel Jean Frontenac
6 Burton On The Water
Calender, Me. 01471

25.____

J. Scott Marsden
174 S. Tipton St.
Cleveland, Ohio

J. Scott Marsden
174 Tipton St.
Cleveland, Ohio

Lawrence T. Haney
171 McDonough St.
Decatur, Ga. 31304

Lawrence T. Haney
171 McDonough St.
Decatur, Ga. 31304

___

KEY (CORRECT ANSWERS)

1.	C		11.	B
2.	A		12.	A
3.	D		13.	C
4.	B		14.	B
5.	A		15.	B
6.	A		16.	C
7.	D		17.	A
8.	C		18.	D
9.	C		19.	A
10.	B		20.	C

21. C
22. C
23. B
24. B
25. C

___

TEST 2

DIRECTIONS: Each question or incomplete statement is followed by several suggested answers or completions. Select the one that BEST answers the question or completes the statement. *PRINT THE LETTER OF THE CORRECT ANSWER IN THE SPACE AT THE RIGHT.*

Questions 1-6.

DIRECTIONS: Questions 1 through 6 are to be answered SOLELY on the basis of the information contained in the following passage.

Duplicating is the process of making a number of identical copies of letters, documents, etc. from an original. Some duplicating processes make copies directly from the original document. Other duplicating processes require the preparation of a special master, and copies are then made from the master. Four of the most common duplicating processes are stencil, fluid, offset, and xerox.

In the stencil process, the typewriter is used to cut the words into a master called a stencil. Drawings, charts, or graphs can be cut into the stencil using a stylus. As many as 3,500 good-quality copies can be reproduced from one stencil. Various grades of finished paper from inexpensive mimeograph to expensive bond can be used.

The fluid process is a good method of copying from 50 to 125 good-quality copies from a master, which is prepared with a special dye. The master is placed on the duplicator, and special paper with a hard finish is moistened and then passed through the duplicator. Some of the dye on the master is dissolved, creating an impression on the paper. The impression becomes lighter as more copies are made; and once the dye on the master is used up, a new master must be made.

The offset process is the most adaptable office duplicating process because this process can be used for making a few copies or many copies. Masters can be made on paper or plastic for a few hundred copies, or on metal plates for as many as 75,000 copies. By using a special technique called photo-offset, charts, photographs, illustrations, or graphs can be reproduced on the master plate. The offset process is capable of producing large quantities of fine, top-quality copies on all types of finished paper.

The xerox process reproduces an exact duplicate from an original. It is the fastest duplicating method because the original material is placed directly on the duplicator, eliminating the need to make a special master. Any kind of paper can be used. The xerox process is the most expensive duplicating process; however, it is the best method of reproducing small quantities of good-quality copies of reports, letters, official documents, memos, or contracts.

1. Of the following, the MOST efficient method of reproducing 5,000 copies of a graph is   1._____

    A. stencil   B. fluid   C. offset   D. xerox

2. The offset process is the MOST adaptable office duplicating process because   2._____

    A. it is the quickest duplicating method
    B. it is the least expensive duplicating method
    C. it can produce a small number or large number of copies
    D. a softer master can be used over and over again

3. Which one of the following duplicating processes uses moistened paper?   3.____

    A. Stencil   B. Fluid   C. Offset   D. Xerox

4. The fluid process would be the BEST process to use for reproducing   4.____

    A. five copies of a school transcript
    B. fifty copies of a memo
    C. five hundred copies of a form letter
    D. five thousand copies of a chart

5. Which one of the following duplicating processes does NOT require a special master?   5.____

    A. Fluid   B. Xerox   C. Offset   D. Stencil

6. Xerox is NOT used for all duplicating jobs because   6.____

    A. it produces poor-quality copies
    B. the process is too expensive
    C. preparing the master is too time-consuming
    D. it cannot produce written reports

7. Assume a city agency has 775 office workers.   7.____
    If 2 out of 25 office workers were absent on a particular day, how many office workers reported to work on that day?

    A. 713   B. 744   C. 750   D. 773

Questions 8-11.

DIRECTIONS: In Questions 8 through 11, select the choice that is CLOSEST in meaning to the underlined word.

SAMPLE: This division reviews the fiscal reports of the agency.
                 In this sentence, the word fiscal means MOST NEARLY
                 A. financial   B. critical   C. basic   D. personnel

          The correct answer is A, financial, because financial is closest to fiscal.

8. A central file eliminates the need to retain duplicate material.   8.____
    The word retain means MOST NEARLY

    A. keep   B. change   C. locate   D. process

9. Filing is a routine office task.   9.____
    Routine means MOST NEARLY

    A. proper   B. regular   C. simple   D. difficult

10. Sometimes a word, phrase, or sentence must be deleted to correct an error.   10.____
    Deleted means MOST NEARLY

    A. removed   B. added   C. expanded   D. improved

11. Your supervisor will <u>evaluate</u> your work.
    <u>Evaluate</u> means MOST NEARLY

    A. judge   B. list   C. assign   D. explain

11._____

Questions 12-19.

DIRECTIONS: The code table below shows 10 letters with matching numbers. For each Question 12 through 19, there are three sets of letters. Each set of letters is followed by a set of numbers which may or may not match their correct letter according to the code table. For each question, check all three sets of letters and numbers and mark your answer:

    A. if no pairs are correctly matched
    B. if only one pair is correctly matched
    C. if only two pairs are correctly matched
    D. if all three pairs are correctly matched

<u>CODE TABLE</u>

T	M	V	D	S	P	R	G	B	H
1	2	3	4	5	6	7	8	9	0

<u>Sample Question:</u>   TMVDSP - 123456
                             RGBHTM - 789011
                             DSPRGB - 256789

In the sample question above, the first set of numbers correctly matches its set of letters. But the second and third pairs contain mistakes. In the second pair, M is incorrectly matched with number 1. According to the code table, letter M should be correctly matched with number 2. In the third pair, the letter D is incorrectly matched with number 2. According to the code table, letter D should be correctly matched with number 4. Since only one of the pairs is correctly matched, the answer to this sample question is B.

12.   RSBMRM - 759262
       GDSRVH - 845730
       VDBRTM - 349713

12._____

13.   TGVSDR - 183247
       SMHRDP - 520647
       TRMHSR - 172057

13._____

14.   DSPRGM - 456782
       MVDBHT - 234902
       HPMDBT - 062491

14._____

15.   BVPTRD - 936184
       GDPHMB - 807029
       GMRHMV - 827032

15._____

16.   MGVRSH - 283750
       TRDMBS - 174295
       SPRMGV - 567283

16._____

17. SGBSDM - 489542
     MGHPTM - 290612
     MPBMHT - 269301

            17._____

18. TDPBHM - 146902
     VPBMRS - 369275
     GDMBHM - 842902

            18._____

19. MVPTBV - 236194
     PDRTMB - 647128
     BGTMSM - 981232

            19._____

Questions 20-25.

DIRECTIONS: In each of Questions 20 through 25, the names of four people are given. For each question, choose as your answer the one of the four names given which should be filed FIRST according to the usual system of alphabetical filing of names, as described in the following paragraph.

In filing names, you must start with the last name. Names are filed in order of the first letter of the last name, then the second letter, etc. Therefore, BAILY would be filed before BROWN, which would be filed before COLT. A name with fewer letters of the same type comes first; i.e., Smith before Smithe. If the last names are the same, the names are filed alphabetically by the first name. If the first name is an initial, a name with an initial would come before a first name that starts with the same letter as the initial. Therefore, I. BROWN would come before IRA BROWN. Finally, if both last name and first name are the same, the name would be filed alphabetically by the middle name, one again an initial coming before a middle name which starts with the same letter as the initial. If there is no middle name at all, the name would come before those with middle initials or names.

<u>Sample Question:</u>   A.   Lester Daniels
                        B.   William Dancer
                        C.   Nathan Danzig
                        D.   Dan Lester

The last names beginning with D are filed before the last name beginning with L. Since DANIELS, DANCER, and DANZIG all begin with the same three letters, you must look at the fourth letter of the last name to determine which name should be filed first. C comes before I or Z in the alphabet, so DANCER is filed before DANIELS or DANZIG. Therefore, the answer to the above sample question is B.

20.   A. Scott Biala   B. Mary Byala   20._____
      C. Martin Baylor   D. Francis Bauer

21.   A. Howard J. Black   B. Howard Black   21._____
      C. J. Howard Black   D. John H. Black

22.   A. Theodora Garth Kingston   B. Theadore Barth Kingston   22._____
      C. Thomas Kingston   D. Thomas T. Kingston

23.   A. Paulette Mary Huerta   B. Paul M. Huerta   23._____
      C. Paulette L. Huerta   D. Peter A. Huerta

24. A. Martha Hunt Morgan B. Martin Hunt Morgan 24.____
     C. Mary H. Morgan D. Martine H. Morgan

25. A. James T. Meerschaum B. James M. Mershum 25.____
     C. James F. Mearshaum D. James N. Meshum

———

KEY (CORRECT ANSWERS)

1.	C	11.	A
2.	C	12.	B
3.	B	13.	B
4.	B	14.	C
5.	B	15.	A
6.	B	16.	D
7.	A	17.	A
8.	A	18.	D
9.	B	19.	A
10.	A	20.	D

21.	B
22.	B
23.	B
24.	A
25.	C

———

TEST 3

DIRECTIONS: Each question or incomplete statement is followed by several suggested answers or completions. Select the one that BEST answers the question or completes the statement. *PRINT THE LETTER OF THE CORRECT ANSWER IN THE SPACE AT THE RIGHT.*

1. Which one of the following statements about proper telephone usage is NOT always cor-   1._____
rect?
   When answering the telephone, you should

   A. know whom you are speaking to
   B. give the caller your undivided attention
   C. identify yourself to the caller
   D. obtain the information the caller wishes before you do your other work

2. Assume that, as a member of a worker's safety committee in your agency, you are   2._____
responsible for encouraging other employees to follow correct safety practices. While you
are working on your regular assignment, you observe an employee violating a safety
rule.
   Of the following, the BEST action for you to take FIRST is to

   A. speak to the employee about safety practices and order him to stop violating the
      safety rule
   B. speak to the employee about safety practices and point out the safety rule he is
      violating
   C. bring the matter up in the next committee meeting
   D. report this violation of the safety rule to the employee's supervisor

3. Assume that you have been temporarily assigned by your supervisor to do a job which   3._____
you do not want to do. The BEST action for you to take is to

   A. discuss the job with your supervisor, explaining why you do not want to do it
   B. discuss the job with your supervisor and tell her that you will not do it
   C. ask a co-worker to take your place on this job
   D. do some other job that you like; your supervisor may give the job you do not like to
      someone else

4. Assume that you keep the confidential personnel files of employees in your unit. A friend   4._____
asks you to obtain some information from the file of one of your co-workers.
   The BEST action to take is to _____ to your friend.

   A. ask the co-worker if you can give the information
   B. ask your supervisor if you can give the information
   C. give the information
   D. refuse to give the information

Questions 5-8.

DIRECTIONS: Questions 5 through 8 are to be answered SOLELY on the basis of the information contained in the following passage.

24

City government is committed to providing a safe and healthy work environment for all city employees. An effective agency safety program reduces accidents by educating employees about the types of careless acts which can cause accidents. Even in an office, accidents can happen. If each employee is aware of possible safety hazards, the number of accidents on the job can be reduced.

Careless use of office equipment can cause accidents and injuries. For example, file cabinet drawers which are filled with papers can be so heavy that the entire cabinet could tip over from the weight of one open drawer.

The bottom drawers of desks and file cabinets should never be left open since employees could easily trip over open drawers and injure themselves.

When reaching for objects on a high shelf, an employee should use a strong, sturdy object such as a step stool to stand on. Makeshift platforms made out of books, papers, or boxes can easily collapse. Even chairs can slide out from under foot, causing serious injury.

Even at an employee's desk, safety hazards can occur. Frayed or cut wires should be repaired or replaced immediately. Computers which are not firmly anchored to the desk or table could fall, causing injury.

Smoking is one of the major causes of fires in the office. A lighted match or improperly extinguished cigarette thrown into a wastebasket filled with paper could cause a major fire with possible loss of life. Where smoking is permitted, ashtrays should be used. Smoking is particularly dangerous in offices where flammable chemicals are used.

5. The goal of an effective safety program is to   5.____

    A. reduce office accidents
    B. stop employees from smoking on the job
    C. encourage employees to continue their education
    D. eliminate high shelves in offices

6. Desks and file cabinets can become safety hazards when   6.____

    A. their drawers are left open
    B. they are used as wastebaskets
    C. they are makeshift
    D. they are not anchored securely to the floor

7. Smoking is especially hazardous when it occurs   7.____

    A. near exposed wires
    B. in a crowded office
    C. in an area where flammable chemicals are used
    D. where books and papers are stored

8. Accidents are likely to occur when   8.____

    A. employees' desks are cluttered with books and papers
    B. employees are not aware of safety hazards
    C. employees close desk drawers
    D. step stools are used to reach high objects

9. Assume that part of your job as a worker in the accounting division of a city agency is to answer the telephone. When you first answer the telephone, it is LEAST important to tell the caller
    9.____

    A. your title   B. your name
    C. the name of your unit   D. the name of your agency

10. Assume that you are assigned to work as a receptionist, and your duties are to answer phones, greet visitors, and do other general office work. You are busy with a routine job when several visitors approach your desk.
    The BEST action to take is to
    10.____

    A. ask the visitors to have a seat and assist them after your work is completed
    B. tell the visitors that you are busy and they should return at a more convenient time
    C. stop working long enough to assist the visitors
    D. continue working and wait for the visitors to ask you for assistance

11. Assume that your supervisor has chosen you to take a special course during working hours to learn a new payroll procedure. Although you know that you were chosen because of your good work record, a co-worker, who feels that he should have been cho-sen, has been telling everyone in your unit that the choice was unfair.
    Of the following, the BEST way to handle this situation FIRST is to
    11.____

    A. suggest to the co-worker that everything in life is unfair
    B. contact your union representative in case your co-worker presents a formal griev-ance
    C. tell your supervisor about your co-worker's complaints and let her handle the situa-tion
    D. tell the co-worker that you were chosen because of your superior work record

12. Assume that while you are working on an assignment which must be completed quickly, a supervisor from another unit asks you to obtain information for her.
    Of the following, the BEST way to respond to her request is to
    12.____

    A. tell her to return in an hour since you are busy
    B. give her the names of some people in her own unit who could help her
    C. tell her you are busy and refer her to a co-worker
    D. tell her that you are busy and ask her if she could wait until you finish your assign-ment

13. A co-worker in your unit is often off from work because of illness. Your supervisor assigns the co-worker's work to you when she is not there. Lately, doing her work has interfered with your own job.
    The BEST action for you to take FIRST is to
    13.____

    A. discuss the problem with your supervisor
    B. complete your own work before starting your co-worker's work
    C. ask other workers in your unit to assist you
    D. work late in order to get the jobs done

26

14. During the month of June, 40,587 people attended a city-owned swimming pool. In July, 13,014 more people attended the swimming pool than the number that had attended in June. In August, 39,655 people attended the swimming pool.
The TOTAL number of people who attended the swimming pool during the months of June, July, and August was

    A. 80,242   B. 93,256   C. 133,843   D. 210,382

14.____

Questions 15-22.

DIRECTIONS: Questions 15 through 22 test how well you understand what you read. It will be necessary for you to read carefully because your answers to these questions must be based ONLY on the information in the following paragraphs.

The telephone directory is made up of two books. The first book consists of the introductory section and the alphabetical listing of names section. The second book is the classified directory (also known as the yellow pages). Many people who are familiar with one book do not realize how useful the other can be. The efficient office worker should become familiar with both books in order to make the best use of this important source of information.

The introductory section gives general instructions for finding numbers in the alphabetical listing and classified directory. This section also explains how to use the telephone company's many services, including the operator and information services, gives examples of charges for local and long-distance calls, and lists area codes for the entire country. In addition, this section provides a useful postal zip code map.

The alphabetical listing of names section lists the names, addresses, and telephone numbers of subscribers in an area. Guide names, or *telltales,* are on the top corner of each page. These guide names indicate the first and last name to be found on that page. *Telltales* help locate any particular name quickly. A cross-reference spelling is also given to help locate names which are spelled several different ways. City, state, and federal government agencies are listed under the major government heading. For example, an agency of the federal government would be listed under *United States Government.*

The classified directory, or yellow pages, is a separate book. In this section are advertising services, public transportation line maps, shopping guides, and listings of businesses arranged by the type of product or services they offer. This book is most useful when looking for the name or phone number of a business when all that is known is the type of product offered and the address, or when trying to locate a particular type of business in an area. Businesses listed in the classified directory can usually be found in the alphabetical listing of names section. When the name of the business is known, you will find the address or phone number more quickly in the alphabetical listing of names section.

15. The introductory section provides

    A. shopping guides   B. government listings
    C. business listings   D. information services

15.____

16. Advertising services would be found in the

    A. introductory section   B. alphabetical listing of names section
    C. classified directory   D. information services

16.____

17. According to the information in the above passage for locating government agencies, the Information Office of the Department of Consumer Affairs of New York City government would be alphabetically listed FIRST under

    A. *I* for Information Offices
    B. *D* for Department of Consumer Affairs
    C. *N* for New York City
    D. *G* for government

17.____

18. When the name of a business is known, the QUICKEST way to find the phone number is to look in the

    A. classified directory
    B. introductory section
    C. alphabetical listing of names section
    D. advertising service section

18.____

19. The QUICKEST way to find the phone number of a business when the type of service a business offers and its address is known is to look in the

    A. classified directory
    B. alphabetical listing of names section
    C. introductory section
    D. information service

19.____

20. What is a *telltale*?

    A. An alphabetical listing
    B. A guide name
    C. A map
    D. A cross-reference listing

20.____

21. The BEST way to find a postal zip code is to look in the

    A. classified directory
    B. introductory section
    C. alphabetical listing of names section
    D. government heading

21.____

22. To help find names which have several different spellings, the telephone directory provides

    A. cross-reference spelling
    B. *telltales*
    C. spelling guides
    D. advertising services

22.____

23. Assume that your agency has been given $2025 to purchase file cabinets. If each file cabinet costs $135, how many file cabinets can your agency purchase?

    A. 8   B. 10   C. 15   D. 16

23.____

24. Assume that your unit ordered 14 staplers at a total cost of $30.20, and each stapler cost the same.
The cost of one stapler was MOST NEARLY

   A. $1.02   B. $1.61   C. $2.16   D. $2.26

24.____

25. Assume that you are responsible for counting and recording licensing fees collected by your department. On a particular day, your department collected in fees 40 checks in the amount of $6 each, 80 checks in the amount of $4 each, 45 twenty dollar bills, 30 ten dollar bills, 42 five dollar bills, and 186 one dollar bills.
The TOTAL amount in fees collected on that day was

   A. $1,406   B. $1,706   C. $2,156   D. $2,356

25.____

26. Assume that you are responsible for your agency's petty cash fund. During the month of February, you pay out 7 $2.00 subway fares and one taxi fare for $10.85. You pay out nothing else from the fund. At the end of February, you count the money left in the fund and find 3 one dollar bills, 4 quarters, 5 dimes, and 4 nickels. The amount of money you had available in the petty cash fund at the BEGINNING of February was

   A. $4.70   B. $16.35   C. $24.85   D. $29.55

26.____

27. You overhear your supervisor criticize a co-worker for handling equipment in an unsafe way. You feel that the criticism may be unfair.
Of the following, it would be BEST for you to

   A. take your co-worker aside and tell her how you feel about your supervisor's comments
   B. interrupt the discussion and defend your co-worker to your supervisor
   C. continue working as if you had not overheard the discussion
   D. make a list of other workers who have violated safety rules and give it to your supervisor

27.____

28. Assume that you have been assigned to work on a long-term project with an employee who is known for being uncooperative.
In beginning to work with this employee, it would be LEAST desirable for you to

   A. understand why the person is uncooperative
   B. act in a calm manner rather than an emotional manner
   C. be appreciative of the co-worker's work
   D. report the co-worker's lack of cooperation to your supervisor

28.____

29. Assume that you are assigned to sell tickets at a city-owned ice skating rink. An adult ticket costs $4.50, and a children's ticket costs $2.25. At the end of a day, you find that you have sold 36 adult tickets and 80 children's tickets.
The TOTAL amount of money you collected for that day was

   A. $244.80   B. $318.00   C. $342.00   D. $348.00

29.____

30. If each office worker files 487 index cards in one hour, how many cards can 26 office workers file in one hour?

   A. 10,662   B. 12,175   C. 12,662   D. 14,266

30.____

KEY (CORRECT ANSWERS)

1.	D		16.	C
2.	B		17.	C
3.	A		18.	C
4.	D		19.	A
5.	A		20.	B
6.	A		21.	B
7.	C		22.	A
8.	B		23.	C
9.	A		24.	C
10.	C		25.	C
11.	C		26.	D
12.	D		27.	C
13.	A		28.	D
14.	C		29.	C
15.	D		30.	C

EXAMINATION SECTION
TEST 1

DIRECTIONS: Each question or incomplete statement is followed by several suggested answers or completions. Select the one that BEST answers the question or completes the statement. *PRINT THE LETTER OF THE CORRECT ANSWER IN THE SPACE AT THE RIGHT.*

1. Assume that a few co-workers meet near your desk and talk about personal matters during working hours. Lately, this practice has interfered with your work.
   In order to stop this practice, the BEST action for you to take FIRST is to

   A. ask your supervisor to put a stop to the co-workers' meeting near your desk
   B. discontinue any friendship with this group
   C. ask your co-workers not to meet near your desk
   D. request that your desk be moved to another location

1.____

2. In order to maintain office coverage during working hours, your supervisor has scheduled your lunch hour from 1 P.M. to 2 P.M. and your co-worker's lunch hour from 12 P.M. to 1 P.M. Lately, your co-worker has been returning late from lunch each day. As a result, you don't get a full hour since you must return to the office by 2 P.M.
   Of the following, the BEST action for you to take FIRST is to

   A. explain to your co-worker in a courteous manner that his lateness is interfering with your right to a full hour for lunch
   B. tell your co-worker that his lateness must stop or you will report him to your supervisor
   C. report your co-worker's lateness to your supervisor
   D. leave at 1 P.M. for lunch, whether your co-worker has returned or not

2.____

3. Assume that, as an office worker, one of your jobs is to open mail sent to your unit, read the mail for content, and send the mail to the appropriate person to handle. You accidentally open and begin to read a letter marked *personal* addressed to a co-worker.
   Of the following, the BEST action for you to take is to

   A. report to your supervisor that your co-worker is receiving personal mail at the office
   B. destroy the letter so that your co-worker does not know you saw it
   C. reseal the letter and place it on the co-worker's desk without saying anything
   D. bring the letter to your co-worker and explain that you opened it by accident

3.____

4. Suppose that in evaluating your work, your supervisor gives you an overall good rating, but states that you sometimes turn in work with careless errors.
   The BEST action for you to take would be to

   A. ask a co-worker who is good at details to proofread your work
   B. take time to do a careful job, paying more attention to detail
   C. continue working as usual since occasional errors are to be expected
   D. ask your supervisor if she would mind correcting your errors

4.____

5. Assume that you are taking a telephone message for a co-worker who is not in the office at the time.
   Of the following, the LEAST important item to write on the message is the

   A. length of the call   B. name of the caller
   C. time of the call   D. telephone number of the caller

5.____

31

Questions 6-13.

DIRECTIONS: Questions 6 through 13 each consist of a sentence which may or may not be an example of good English. The underlined parts of each sentence may be correct or incorrect. Examine each sentence, considering grammar, punctuation, spelling, and capitalization. If the English usage in the underlined parts of the sentence given is better than any of the changes in the underlined words suggested in Options B, C, or D, choose Option A. If the changes in the underlined words suggested in Options B, C, or D would make the sentence correct, choose the correct option. Do not choose an option that will change the meaning of the sentence.

6. This <u>Fall</u>, the office will be closed on <u>Columbus Day, October</u> 9th.   6._____

    A. Correct as is
    B. fall...Columbus Day, October
    C. Fall...columbus day, October
    D. fall...Columbus Day, october

7. This manual <u>discribes the duties performed</u> by an Office Aide.   7._____

    A. Correct as is
    B. describe the duties performed
    C. discribe the duties performed
    D. describes the duties performed

8. There <u>weren't no</u> paper in the supply closet.   8._____

    A. Correct as is   B. weren't any
    C. wasn't any   D. wasn't no

9. The new employees left <u>there</u> office to attend a meeting.   9._____

    A. Correct as is   B. they're
    C. their   D. thier

10. The office worker started working at <u>8:30 a.m.</u>   10._____

    A. Correct as is   B. 8:30 a.m.
    C. 8;30 a,m.   D. 8:30 am

11. The <u>alphabet, or A to Z sequence</u> are the basis of most filing systems.   11._____

    A. Correct as is
    B. alphabet, or A to Z sequence, is
    C. alphabet, or A to Z sequence are
    D. alphabet, or A too Z sequence, is

12. <u>Those</u> file cabinets are five <u>feet</u> tall.   12._____

    A. Correct as is   B. Them...feet
    C. Those...foot   D. Them...foot

13. The Office Aide checked the <u>register and finding</u> the date of the meeting.　　13.____

    A.　Correct as is　　　　　　　　　B.　regaster and finding
    C.　register and found　　　　　　　D.　regaster and found

Questions 14-21.

DIRECTIONS:　Each of Questions 14 through 21 has two lists of numbers. Each list contains three sets of numbers. Check each of the three sets in the list on the right to see if they are the same as the corresponding set in the list on the left. Mark your answers:
    A.　If none of the sets in the right list are the same as those in the left list
    B.　if only one of the sets in the right list are the same as those in the left list
    C.　if only two of the sets in the right list are the same as those in the left list
    D.　if all three sets in the right list are the same as those in the left list

14.　7354183476　　　　　　7354983476　　　　　14.____
　　　4474747744　　　　　　4474747774
　　　57914302311　　　　　57914302311

15.　7143592185　　　　　　7143892185　　　　　15.____
　　　8344517699　　　　　　8344518699
　　　9178531263　　　　　　9178531263

16.　2572114731　　　　　　257214731　　　　　16.____
　　　8806835476　　　　　　8806835476
　　　8255831246　　　　　　8255831246

17.　331476853821　　　　331476858621　　　17.____
　　　6976658532996　　　6976655832996
　　　3766042113715　　　3766042113745

18.　8806663315　　　　　　8806663315　　　　　18.____
　　　74477138449　　　　　74477138449
　　　211756663666　　　　211756663666

19.　990006966996　　　　99000696996　　　　19.____
　　　53022219743　　　　　53022219843
　　　4171171117717　　　4171171177717

20.　24400222433004　　24400222433004　　20.____
　　　5300030055000355　5300030055500355
　　　20000075532002022　20000075532002022

21.　611166640660001116　61116664066001116　21.____
　　　7111300117001100733　7111300117001100733
　　　26666446664476518　26666446664476518

33

Questions 22-25.

DIRECTIONS: Each of Questions 22 through 25 has two lists of names and addresses. Each list contains three sets of names and addresses. Check each of the three sets in the list on the right to see if they are the same as the corresponding set in the list on the left. Mark your answers:
- A. if none of the sets in the right list are the same as those in the left list
- B. if only one of the sets in the right list is the same as those in the left list
- C. if only two of the sets in the right list are the same as those in the left list
- D. if all three sets in the right list are the same as those in the left list

22. Mary T. Berlinger
2351 Hampton St.
Monsey, N.Y. 20117

Eduardo Benes
473 Kingston Avenue
Central Islip, N.Y. 11734

Alan Carrington Fuchs
17 Gnarled Hollow Road
Los Angeles, CA 91635

Mary T. Berlinger
2351 Hampton St.
Monsey, N.Y. 20117

Eduardo Benes
473 Kingston Avenue
Central Islip, N.Y. 11734

Alan Carrington Fuchs
17 Gnarled Hollow Road
Los Angeles, CA 91685

22._____

23. David John Jacobson
178 35 St. Apt. 4C
New York, N.Y. 00927

Ann-Marie Calonella
7243 South Ridge Blvd.
Bakersfield, CA 96714

Pauline M. Thompson
872 Linden Ave.
Houston, Texas 70321

David John Jacobson
178 53 St. Apt. 4C
New York, N.Y. 00927

Ann-Marie Calonella
7243 South Ridge Blvd.
Bakersfield, CA 96714

Pauline M. Thomson
872 Linden Ave.
Houston, Texas 70321

23._____

24. Chester LeRoy Masterton
152 Lacy Rd.
Kankakee, Ill. 54532

William Maloney
S. LaCrosse Pla.
Wausau, Wisconsin 52146

Cynthia V. Barnes
16 Pines Rd.
Greenpoint, Miss. 20376

Chester LeRoy Masterson
152 Lacy Rd.
Kankakee, Ill. 54532

William Maloney
S. LaCross Pla.
Wausau, Wisconsin 52146

Cynthia V. Barnes
16 Pines Rd.
Greenpoint, Miss. 20376

24._____

25.   Marcel Jean Frontenac   Marcel Jean Frontenac   25.____
       6 Burton On The Water   6 Burton On The Water
       Calender, Me. 01471   Calender, Me. 01471

       J. Scott Marsden   J. Scott Marsden
       174 S. Tipton St.   174 Tipton St.
       Cleveland, Ohio   Cleveland, Ohio

       Lawrence T. Haney   Lawrence T. Haney
       171 McDonough St.   171 McDonough St.
       Decatur, Ga. 31304   Decatur, Ga. 31304

KEY (CORRECT ANSWERS)

1.	C		11.	B
2.	A		12.	A
3.	D		13.	C
4.	B		14.	B
5.	A		15.	B
6.	A		16.	C
7.	D		17.	A
8.	C		18.	D
9.	C		19.	A
10.	B		20.	C

21.	C
22.	C
23.	B
24.	B
25.	C

TEST 2

DIRECTIONS: Each question or incomplete statement is followed by several suggested answers or completions. Select the one that BEST answers the question or completes the statement. *PRINT THE LETTER OF THE CORRECT ANSWER IN THE SPACE AT THE RIGHT.*

Questions 1-6.

DIRECTIONS: Questions 1 through 6 are to be answered SOLELY on the basis of the information contained in the following passage.

Duplicating is the process of making a number of identical copies of letters, documents, etc. from an original. Some duplicating processes make copies directly from the original document. Other duplicating processes require the preparation of a special master, and copies are then made from the master. Four of the most common duplicating processes are stencil, fluid, offset, and xerox.

In the stencil process, the typewriter is used to cut the words into a master called a stencil. Drawings, charts, or graphs can be cut into the stencil using a stylus. As many as 3,500 good-quality copies can be reproduced from one stencil. Various grades of finished paper from inexpensive mimeograph to expensive bond can be used.

The fluid process is a good method of copying from 50 to 125 good-quality copies from a master, which is prepared with a special dye. The master is placed on the duplicator, and special paper with a hard finish is moistened and then passed through the duplicator. Some of the dye on the master is dissolved, creating an impression on the paper. The impression becomes lighter as more copies are made; and once the dye on the master is used up, a new master must be made.

The offset process is the most adaptable office duplicating process because this process can be used for making a few copies or many copies. Masters can be made on paper or plastic for a few hundred copies, or on metal plates for as many as 75,000 copies. By using a special technique called photo-offset, charts, photographs, illustrations, or graphs can be reproduced on the master plate. The offset process is capable of producing large quantities of fine, top-quality copies on all types of finished paper.

The xerox process reproduces an exact duplicate from an original. It is the fastest duplicating method because the original material is placed directly on the duplicator, eliminating the need to make a special master. Any kind of paper can be used. The xerox process is the most expensive duplicating process; however, it is the best method of reproducing small quantities of good-quality copies of reports, letters, official documents, memos, or contracts.

1. Of the following, the MOST efficient method of reproducing 5,000 copies of a graph is   1._____

   A. stencil   B. fluid   C. offset   D. xerox

2. The offset process is the MOST adaptable office duplicating process because   2._____

   A. it is the quickest duplicating method
   B. it is the least expensive duplicating method
   C. it can produce a small number or large number of copies
   D. a softer master can be used over and over again

3. Which one of the following duplicating processes uses moistened paper?   3.____

    A.   Stencil   B.   Fluid   C.   Offset   D.   Xerox

4. The fluid process would be the BEST process to use for reproducing   4.____

    A.   five copies of a school transcript
    B.   fifty copies of a memo
    C.   five hundred copies of a form letter
    D.   five thousand copies of a chart

5. Which one of the following duplicating processes does NOT require a special master?   5.____

    A.   Fluid   B.   Xerox   C.   Offset   D.   Stencil

6. Xerox is NOT used for all duplicating jobs because   6.____

    A.   it produces poor-quality copies
    B.   the process is too expensive
    C.   preparing the master is too time-consuming
    D.   it cannot produce written reports

7. Assume a city agency has 775 office workers.   7.____
If 2 out of 25 office workers were absent on a particular day, how many office workers reported to work on that day?

    A.   713   B.   744   C.   750   D.   773

Questions 8-11.

DIRECTIONS: In Questions 8 through 11, select the choice that is CLOSEST in meaning to the underlined word.

SAMPLE: This division reviews the fiscal reports of the agency.
In this sentence, the word fiscal means MOST NEARLY
    A.   financial   B.   critical   C.   basic   D.   personnel

The correct answer is A, financial, because financial is closest to fiscal.

8. A central file eliminates the need to retain duplicate material.   8.____
The word retain means MOST NEARLY

    A.   keep   B.   change   C.   locate   D.   process

9. Filing is a routine office task.   9.____
Routine means MOST NEARLY

    A.   proper   B.   regular   C.   simple   D.   difficult

10. Sometimes a word, phrase, or sentence must be deleted to correct an error.   10.____
Deleted means MOST NEARLY

    A.   removed   B.   added   C.   expanded   D.   improved

11. Your supervisor will <u>evaluate</u> your work.
    <u>Evaluate</u> means MOST NEARLY

11.____

    A. judge   B. list   C. assign   D. explain

Questions 12-19.

DIRECTIONS: The code table below shows 10 letters with matching numbers. For each Question 12 through 19, there are three sets of letters. Each set of letters is followed by a set of numbers which may or may not match their correct letter according to the code table. For each question, check all three sets of letters and numbers and mark your answer:
    A.   if no pairs are correctly matched
    B.   if only one pair is correctly matched
    C.   if only two pairs are correctly matched
    D.   if all three pairs are correctly matched

<u>CODE TABLE</u>

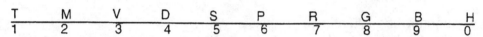

T	M	V	D	S	P	R	G	B	H
1	2	3	4	5	6	7	8	9	0

<u>Sample Question:</u>   TMVDSP - 123456
                        RGBHTM - 789011
                        DSPRGB - 256789

In the sample question above, the first set of numbers correctly matches its set of letters. But the second and third pairs contain mistakes. In the second pair, M is incorrectly matched with number 1. According to the code table, letter M should be correctly matched with number 2. In the third pair, the letter D is incorrectly matched with number 2. According to the code table, letter D should be correctly matched with number 4. Since only one of the pairs is correctly matched, the answer to this sample question is B.

12. RSBMRM - 759262
    GDSRVH - 845730
    VDBRTM - 349713

12.____

13. TGVSDR - 183247
    SMHRDP - 520647
    TRMHSR - 172057

13.____

14. DSPRGM - 456782
    MVDBHT - 234902
    HPMDBT - 062491

14.____

15. BVPTRD - 936184
    GDPHMB - 807029
    GMRHMV - 827032

15.____

16. MGVRSH - 283750
    TRDMBS - 174295
    SPRMGV - 567283

16.____

17. SGBSDM - 489542   17.____
    MGHPTM - 290612
    MPBMHT - 269301

18. TDPBHM - 146902   18.____
    VPBMRS - 369275
    GDMBHM - 842902

19. MVPTBV - 236194   19.____
    PDRTMB - 647128
    BGTMSM - 981232

Questions 20-25.

DIRECTIONS: In each of Questions 20 through 25, the names of four people are given. For
               each question, choose as your answer the one of the four names given which
               should be filed FIRST according to the usual system of alphabetical filing of
               names, as described in the following paragraph.

In filing names, you must start with the last name. Names are filed in order of the first letter of the last name, then the second letter, etc. Therefore, BAILY would be filed before
BROWN, which would be filed before COLT. A name with fewer letters of the same type
comes first; i.e., Smith before Smithe. If the last names are the same, the names are filed
alphabetically by the first name. If the first name is an initial, a name with an initial would
come before a first name that starts with the same letter as the initial. Therefore, I. BROWN
would come before IRA BROWN. Finally, if both last name and first name are the same, the
name would be filed alphabetically by the middle name, one again an initial coming before a
middle name which starts with the same letter as the initial. If there is no middle name at all,
the name would come before those with middle initials or names.

Sample Question: A.   Lester Daniels
                    B.   William Dancer
                    C.   Nathan Danzig
                    D.   Dan Lester

The last names beginning with D are filed before the last name beginning with L. Since
DANIELS, DANCER, and DANZIG all begin with the same three letters, you must look at the
fourth letter of the last name to determine which name should be filed first. C comes before I or
Z in the alphabet, so DANCER is filed before DANIELS or DANZIG. Therefore, the answer to
the above sample question is B.

20. A. Scott Biala   B. Mary Byala   20.____
     C. Martin Baylor   D. Francis Bauer

21. A. Howard J. Black   B. Howard Black   21.____
     C. J. Howard Black   D. John H. Black

22. A. Theodora Garth Kingston B. Theadore Barth Kingston   22.____
     C. Thomas Kingston   D. Thomas T. Kingston

23. A. Paulette Mary Huerta   B. Paul M. Huerta   23.____
     C. Paulette L. Huerta   D. Peter A. Huerta

24. A. Martha Hunt Morgan   B. Martin Hunt Morgan   24.____
     C. Mary H. Morgan   D. Martine H. Morgan

25. A. James T. Meerschaum   B. James M. Mershum   25.____
     C. James F. Mearshaum   D. James N. Meshum

———

KEY (CORRECT ANSWERS)

1.	C	11.	A
2.	C	12.	B
3.	B	13.	B
4.	B	14.	C
5.	B	15.	A
6.	B	16.	D
7.	A	17.	A
8.	A	18.	D
9.	B	19.	A
10.	A	20.	D

21.	B
22.	B
23.	B
24.	A
25.	C

———

TEST 3

DIRECTIONS: Each question or incomplete statement is followed by several suggested answers or completions. Select the one that BEST answers the question or completes the statement. *PRINT THE LETTER OF THE CORRECT ANSWER IN THE SPACE AT THE RIGHT.*

1. Which one of the following statements about proper telephone usage is NOT always correct?
   When answering the telephone, you should

   A. know whom you are speaking to
   B. give the caller your undivided attention
   C. identify yourself to the caller
   D. obtain the information the caller wishes before you do your other work

   1.____

2. Assume that, as a member of a worker's safety committee in your agency, you are responsible for encouraging other employees to follow correct safety practices. While you are working on your regular assignment, you observe an employee violating a safety rule.
   Of the following, the BEST action for you to take FIRST is to

   A. speak to the employee about safety practices and order him to stop violating the safety rule
   B. speak to the employee about safety practices and point out the safety rule he is violating
   C. bring the matter up in the next committee meeting
   D. report this violation of the safety rule to the employee's supervisor

   2.____

3. Assume that you have been temporarily assigned by your supervisor to do a job which you do not want to do. The BEST action for you to take is to

   A. discuss the job with your supervisor, explaining why you do not want to do it
   B. discuss the job with your supervisor and tell her that you will not do it
   C. ask a co-worker to take your place on this job
   D. do some other job that you like; your supervisor may give the job you do not like to someone else

   3.____

4. Assume that you keep the confidential personnel files of employees in your unit. A friend asks you to obtain some information from the file of one of your co-workers.
   The BEST action to take is to _____ to your friend.

   A. ask the co-worker if you can give the information
   B. ask your supervisor if you can give the information
   C. give the information
   D. refuse to give the information

   4.____

Questions 5-8.

DIRECTIONS: Questions 5 through 8 are to be answered SOLELY on the basis of the information contained in the following passage.

City government is committed to providing a safe and healthy work environment for all city employees. An effective agency safety program reduces accidents by educating employees about the types of careless acts which can cause accidents. Even in an office, accidents can happen. If each employee is aware of possible safety hazards, the number of accidents on the job can be reduced.

Careless use of office equipment can cause accidents and injuries. For example, file cabinet drawers which are filled with papers can be so heavy that the entire cabinet could tip over from the weight of one open drawer.

The bottom drawers of desks and file cabinets should never be left open since employees could easily trip over open drawers and injure themselves.

When reaching for objects on a high shelf, an employee should use a strong, sturdy object such as a step stool to stand on. Makeshift platforms made out of books, papers, or boxes can easily collapse. Even chairs can slide out from under foot, causing serious injury.

Even at an employee's desk, safety hazards can occur. Frayed or cut wires should be repaired or replaced immediately. Computers which are not firmly anchored to the desk or table could fall, causing injury.

Smoking is one of the major causes of fires in the office. A lighted match or improperly extinguished cigarette thrown into a wastebasket filled with paper could cause a major fire with possible loss of life. Where smoking is permitted, ashtrays should be used. Smoking is particularly dangerous in offices where flammable chemicals are used.

5. The goal of an effective safety program is to   5._____

     A.   reduce office accidents
     B.   stop employees from smoking on the job
     C.   encourage employees to continue their education
     D.   eliminate high shelves in offices

6. Desks and file cabinets can become safety hazards when   6._____

     A.   their drawers are left open
     B.   they are used as wastebaskets
     C.   they are makeshift
     D.   they are not anchored securely to the floor

7. Smoking is especially hazardous when it occurs   7._____

     A.   near exposed wires
     B.   in a crowded office
     C.   in an area where flammable chemicals are used
     D.   where books and papers are stored

8. Accidents are likely to occur when   8._____

     A.   employees' desks are cluttered with books and papers
     B.   employees are not aware of safety hazards
     C.   employees close desk drawers
     D.   step stools are used to reach high objects

9. Assume that part of your job as a worker in the accounting division of a city agency is to answer the telephone. When you first answer the telephone, it is LEAST important to tell the caller

    A. your title   B. your name
    C. the name of your unit   D. the name of your agency

    9.____

10. Assume that you are assigned to work as a receptionist, and your duties are to answer phones, greet visitors, and do other general office work. You are busy with a routine job when several visitors approach your desk.
The BEST action to take is to

    A. ask the visitors to have a seat and assist them after your work is completed
    B. tell the visitors that you are busy and they should return at a more convenient time
    C. stop working long enough to assist the visitors
    D. continue working and wait for the visitors to ask you for assistance

    10.____

11. Assume that your supervisor has chosen you to take a special course during working hours to learn a new payroll procedure. Although you know that you were chosen because of your good work record, a co-worker, who feels that he should have been chosen, has been telling everyone in your unit that the choice was unfair.
Of the following, the BEST way to handle this situation FIRST is to

    A. suggest to the co-worker that everything in life is unfair
    B. contact your union representative in case your co-worker presents a formal grievance
    C. tell your supervisor about your co-worker's complaints and let her handle the situation
    D. tell the co-worker that you were chosen because of your superior work record

    11.____

12. Assume that while you are working on an assignment which must be completed quickly, a supervisor from another unit asks you to obtain information for her.
Of the following, the BEST way to respond to her request is to

    A. tell her to return in an hour since you are busy
    B. give her the names of some people in her own unit who could help her
    C. tell her you are busy and refer her to a co-worker
    D. tell her that you are busy and ask her if she could wait until you finish your assignment

    12.____

13. A co-worker in your unit is often off from work because of illness. Your supervisor assigns the co-worker's work to you when she is not there. Lately, doing her work has interfered with your own job.
The BEST action for you to take FIRST is to

    A. discuss the problem with your supervisor
    B. complete your own work before starting your co-worker's work
    C. ask other workers in your unit to assist you
    D. work late in order to get the jobs done

    13.____

14. During the month of June, 40,587 people attended a city-owned swimming pool. In July, 13,014 more people attended the swimming pool than the number that had attended in June. In August, 39,655 people attended the swimming pool.
The TOTAL number of people who attended the swimming pool during the months of June, July, and August was   14._____

    A. 80,242   B. 93,256   C. 133,843   D. 210,382

Questions 15-22.

DIRECTIONS: Questions 15 through 22 test how well you understand what you read. It will be necessary for you to read carefully because your answers to these questions must be based ONLY on the information in the following paragraphs.

The telephone directory is made up of two books. The first book consists of the introductory section and the alphabetical listing of names section. The second book is the classified directory (also known as the yellow pages). Many people who are familiar with one book do not realize how useful the other can be. The efficient office worker should become familiar with both books in order to make the best use of this important source of information.

The introductory section gives general instructions for finding numbers in the alphabetical listing and classified directory. This section also explains how to use the telephone company's many services, including the operator and information services, gives examples of charges for local and long-distance calls, and lists area codes for the entire country. In addition, this section provides a useful postal zip code map.

The alphabetical listing of names section lists the names, addresses, and telephone numbers of subscribers in an area. Guide names, or *telltales,* are on the top corner of each page. These guide names indicate the first and last name to be found on that page. *Telltales* help locate any particular name quickly. A cross-reference spelling is also given to help locate names which are spelled several different ways. City, state, and federal government agencies are listed under the major government heading. For example, an agency of the federal government would be listed under *United States Government.*

The classified directory, or yellow pages, is a separate book. In this section are advertising services, public transportation line maps, shopping guides, and listings of businesses arranged by the type of product or services they offer. This book is most useful when looking for the name or phone number of a business when all that is known is the type of product offered and the address, or when trying to locate a particular type of business in an area. Businesses listed in the classified directory can usually be found in the alphabetical listing of names section. When the name of the business is known, you will find the address or phone number more quickly in the alphabetical listing of names section.

15. The introductory section provides   15._____

    A. shopping guides   B. government listings
    C. business listings   D. information services

16. Advertising services would be found in the   16._____

    A. introductory section   B. alphabetical listing of names section
    C. classified directory   D. information services

17. According to the information in the above passage for locating government agencies, the   17._____
Information Office of the Department of Consumer Affairs of New York City government
would be alphabetically listed FIRST under

    A.   *I* for Information Offices
    B.   *D* for Department of Consumer Affairs
    C.   *N* for New York City
    D.   *G* for government

18. When the name of a business is known, the QUICKEST way to find the phone number is   18.___ _
to look in the

    A.   classified directory
    B.   introductory section
    C.   alphabetical listing of names section
    D.   advertising service section

19. The QUICKEST way to find the phone number of a business when the type of service a   19._____
business offers and its address is known is to look in the

    A.   classified directory
    B.   alphabetical listing of names section
    C.   introductory section
    D.   information service

20. What is a *telltale*?   20._____

    A.   An alphabetical listing
    B.   A guide name
    C.   A map
    D.   A cross-reference listing

21. The BEST way to find a postal zip code is to look in the   21._____

    A.   classified directory
    B.   introductory section
    C.   alphabetical listing of names section
    D.   government heading

22. To help find names which have several different spellings, the telephone directory pro-   22._____
vides

    A.   cross-reference spelling   B.   *telltales*
    C.   spelling guides   D.   advertising services

23. Assume that your agency has been given $2025 to purchase file cabinets.   23._____
If each file cabinet costs $135, how many file cabinets can your agency purchase?

    A. 8   B. 10   C. 15   D. 16

24. Assume that your unit ordered 14 staplers at a total cost of $30.20, and each stapler cost the same.
The cost of one stapler was MOST NEARLY 24.____

    A. $1.02   B. $1.61   C. $2.16   D. $2.26

25. Assume that you are responsible for counting and recording licensing fees collected by your department. On a particular day, your department collected in fees 40 checks in the amount of $6 each, 80 checks in the amount of $4 each, 45 twenty dollar bills, 30 ten dollar bills, 42 five dollar bills, and 186 one dollar bills.
The TOTAL amount in fees collected on that day was 25.____

    A. $1,406   B. $1,706   C. $2,156   D. $2,356

26. Assume that you are responsible for your agency's petty cash fund. During the month of February, you pay out 7 $2.00 subway fares and one taxi fare for $10.85. You pay out nothing else from the fund. At the end of February, you count the money left in the fund and find 3 one dollar bills, 4 quarters, 5 dimes, and 4 nickels. The amount of money you had available in the petty cash fund at the BEGINNING of February was 26.____

    A. $4.70   B. $16.35   C. $24.85   D. $29.55

27. You overhear your supervisor criticize a co-worker for handling equipment in an unsafe way. You feel that the criticism may be unfair.
Of the following, it would be BEST for you to 27.____

    A. take your co-worker aside and tell her how you feel about your supervisor's comments
    B. interrupt the discussion and defend your co-worker to your supervisor
    C. continue working as if you had not overheard the discussion
    D. make a list of other workers who have violated safety rules and give it to your supervisor

28. Assume that you have been assigned to work on a long-term project with an employee who is known for being uncooperative.
In beginning to work with this employee, it would be LEAST desirable for you to 28.____

    A. understand why the person is uncooperative
    B. act in a calm manner rather than an emotional manner
    C. be appreciative of the co-worker's work
    D. report the co-worker's lack of cooperation to your supervisor

29. Assume that you are assigned to sell tickets at a city-owned ice skating rink. An adult ticket costs $4.50, and a children's ticket costs $2.25. At the end of a day, you find that you have sold 36 adult tickets and 80 children's tickets.
The TOTAL amount of money you collected for that day was 29.____

    A. $244.80   B. $318.00   C. $342.00   D. $348.00

30. If each office worker files 487 index cards in one hour, how many cards can 26 office workers file in one hour? 30.____

    A. 10,662   B. 12,175   C. 12,662   D. 14,266

KEY (CORRECT ANSWERS)

1.	D	16.	C
2.	B	17.	C
3.	A	18.	C
4.	D	19.	A
5.	A	20.	B
6.	A	21.	B
7.	C	22.	A
8.	B	23.	C
9.	A	24.	C
10.	C	25.	C
11.	C	26.	D
12.	D	27.	C
13.	A	28.	D
14.	C	29.	C
15.	D	30.	C

———

EXAMINATION SECTION
TEST 1

DIRECTIONS: Each question or incomplete statement is followed by several suggested answers or completions. Select the one that BEST answers the question or completes the statement. *PRINT THE LETTER OF THE CORRECT ANSWER IN THE SPACE AT THE RIGHT.*

1. If you open a personal letter by mistake, the one of the following actions which it would generally be BEST for you to take is to

    A. ignore your error, attach the envelope to the letter, and distribute in the usual manner
    B. personally give the addressee the letter without any explanation
    C. place the letter inside the envelope, indicate under your initials that it was opened in error, and give to the addressee
    D. reseal the envelope or place the contents in another envelope and pass on to addressee

1.____

2. If you receive a telephone call regarding a matter which your office does not handle, you should FIRST

    A. give the caller the telephone number of the proper office so that he can dial again
    B. offer to transfer the caller to the proper office
    C. suggest that the caller re-dial since he probably dialed incorrectly
    D. tell the caller he has reached the wrong office and then hang up

2.____

3. When you answer the telephone, the MOST important reason for identifying yourself and your organization is to

    A. give the caller time to collect his or her thoughts
    B. impress the caller with your courtesy
    C. inform the caller that he or she has reached the right number
    D. set a business-like tone at the beginning of the conversation

3.____

4. The one of the following cases in which you would NOT place a special notation in the left margin of a letter that you have typed is when

    A. one of the copies is intended for someone other than the addressee of the letter
    B. you enclose a flyer with the letter
    C. you sign your superior's name to the letter, at his or her request
    D. the letter refers to something being sent under separate cover

4.____

5. Suppose that you accidentally cut a letter or enclosure as you are opening an envelope with a paper knife.
The one of the following that you should do FIRST is to

    A. determine whether the document is important
    B. clip or staple the pieces together and process as usual
    C. mend the cut document with transparent tape
    D. notify the sender that the communication was damaged and request another copy

5.____

6. As soon as you pick up the phone, a very angry caller begins immediately to complain about city agencies and *red tape*. He says that he has been shifted to two or three different offices. It turns out that he is seeking information which is not immediately available to you. You believe you know, however, where it can be found.
Which of the following actions is the BEST one for you to take?

    A. To eliminate all confusion, suggest that the caller write the mayor stating explicitly what he wants.
    B. Apologize by telling the caller how busy city agencies now are, but also tell him directly that you do not have the information he needs.
    C. Ask for the caller's telephone number, and assure him you will call back after you have checked further.
    D. Give the caller the name and telephone number of the person who might be able to help, but explain that you are not positive he will get results.

7. Suppose that one of your duties is to dictate responses to routine requests from the public for information. A letter writer asks for information which, as expressed in a one-sentence, explicit agency rule, cannot be given out to the public.
Of the following ways of answering the letter, which is the MOST efficient?

    A. Quote verbatim that section of the agency rules which prohibits giving this information to the public.
    B. Without quoting the rule, explain why you cannot accede to the request and suggest alternative sources.
    C. Describe how carefully the request was considered before classifying it as subject to the rule forbidding the issuance of such information.
    D. Acknowledge receipt of the letter and advise that the requested information is not released to the public.

8. Suppose you assist in supervising a staff which has rather high morale, and your own supervisor asks you to poll the staff to find out who will be able to work overtime this particular evening to help complete emergency work.
Which of the following approaches would be MOST likely to win their cooperation while maintaining their morale?

    A. Tell them that the better assignments will be given only to those who work overtime.
    B. Tell them that occasional overtime is a job requirement.
    C. Assure them they'll be doing you a personal favor.
    D. Let them know clearly why the overtime is needed.

9. Suppose that you have been asked to write and to prepare for reproduction new departmental vacation leave regulations.
After you have written the new regulations, all of which fit on two pages, which one of the following would be the BEST method of reproducing 1,000 copies?

    A. An outside private printer because you can best maintain confidentiality using this technique
    B. Photocopying because the copies will have the best possible appearance
    C. Sending the file to all department employees as printable PDFs
    D. Printing and collating on the office high-volume printer

10. You are in charge of verifying employees' qualifications. This involves telephoning previous employers and schools. One of the applications which you are reviewing contains
information which you are almost certain is correct on the basis of what the employee
has told you.
The BEST thing to do is to

    A. check the information again with the employer
    B. perform the required verification procedures
    C. accept the information as valid
    D. ask a superior to verify the information

10.____

11. The practice of immediately identifying oneself and one's place of employment when
contacting persons on the telephone is

    A. *good* because the receiver of the call can quickly identify the caller and establish a
frame of reference
    B. *good* because it helps to set the caller at ease with the other party
    C. *poor* because it is not necessary to divulge that information when making general
calls
    D. *poor* because it takes longer to arrive at the topic to be discussed

11.____

12. Which one of the following should be the MOST important overall consideration when
preparing a recommendation to automate a large-scale office activity?
The

    A. number of models of automated equipment available
    B. benefits and costs of automation
    C. fears and resistance of affected employees
    D. experience of offices which have automated similar activities

12.____

13. A tickler file is MOST appropriate for filing materials

    A. chronologically according to date they were received
    B. alphabetically by name
    C. alphabetically by subject
    D. chronologically according to date they should be followed up

13.____

14. Which of the following is the BEST reason for decentralizing rather then centralizing the
use of duplicating machines?

    A. Developing and retaining efficient duplicating machine operators
    B. Facilitating supervision of duplicating services
    C. Motivating employees to produce legible duplicated copies
    D. Placing the duplicating machines where they are most convenient and most fre-
quently used

14.____

15. Window envelopes are sometimes considered preferable to individually addressed envelopes PRIMARILY because

    A. window envelopes are available in standard sizes for all purposes
    B. window envelopes are more attractive and official-looking
    C. the use of window envelopes eliminates the risk of inserting a letter in the wrong
envelope
    D. the use of window envelopes requires neater typing

15.____

16. In planning the layout of a new office, the utilization of space and the arrangement of staff, furnishings, and equipment should usually be MOST influenced by the

    A. gross square footage
    B. status differences in the chain of command
    C. framework of informal relationships among employees
    D. activities to be performed

16.____

17. Office forms sometimes consist of several copies, each of a different color. The MAIN reason for using different colors is to

    A. make a favorable impression on the users of the form
    B. distinguish each copy from the others
    C. facilitate the preparation of legible carbon copies
    D. reduce cost, since using colored stock permits recycling of paper

17.____

18. Which of the following is the BEST justification for obtaining a photocopying machine for the office?

    A. A photocopying machine can produce an unlimited number of copies at a low fixed cost per copy.
    B. Employees need little training in operating a photocopying machine.
    C. Office costs will be reduced and efficiency increased.
    D. The legibility of a photocopy generally is superior to copy produced by any other office duplicating device.

18.____

19. An administrative officer in charge of a small fund for buying office supplies has just written a check to Charles Laird, a supplier, and has sent the check by messenger to him. A half-hour later, the messenger telephones the administrative officer. He has lost the check.
Which of the following is the MOST important action for the administrative officer to take under these circumstances?

    A. Ask the messenger to return and write a report describing the loss of the check.
    B. Make a note on the performance record of the messenger who lost the check.
    C. Take the necessary steps to have payment stopped on the check.
    D. Refrain from doing anything since the check may be found shortly.

19.____

20. A petty cash fund is set up PRIMARILY to

    A. take care of small investments that must be made from time to time
    B. take care of small expenses that arise from time to time
    C. provide a fund to be used as the office wants to use it with little need to maintain records
    D. take care of expenses that develop during emergencies such as machine break-downs and fires

20.____

21. Your superior has asked you to send a package from your agency to a government agency in another city. He has written out the message and has indicated the name of the government agency.
When you prepare the package for mailing, which of the following items that your superior has not mentioned must you be sure to include?

21.____

A. Today's date
B. The full address of the government agency
C. A polite opening such as *Dear Sirs*
D. A final sentence such as *We would appreciate hearing from your agency in reply as soon as is convenient for you*

22. In addition to the original piece of correspondence, one should USUALLY also have typed

22.____

    A. a single copy
    B. as many copies as can be typed at one time
    C. no more copies than are needed
    D. two copies

23. The one of the following which is the BEST procedure to follow when making a short insert in a completed dictation is to

23.____

    A. label the insert with a letter and indicate the position of the insert in the text by writing the identifying letter in the proper place
    B. squeeze the insert into its proper place within the main text of the dictation
    C. take down the insert and check the placement with the person who dictated when you are ready to transcribe your notes
    D. transcribe the dictation into longhand, including the insert in its proper position

24. The one of the following procedures which will be MOST efficient in helping you to quickly open your dictation notebook to a clean sheet is to

24.____

    A. clip or place a rubberband around the used portion of the notebook
    B. leave the book out and open to a clean page when not in use
    C. transcribe each dictation after it is given and rip out the used pages
    D. use a book marker to indicate which portion of the notebook has been used

25. The purpose of dating your dictation notebooks is GENERALLY to

25.____

    A. enable you to easily refer to your notes at a later date
    B. ensure that you transcribe your notes in the order in which they were dictated
    C. set up a precise record-keeping procedure
    D. show your employer that you pay attention to detail

KEY (CORRECT ANSWERS)

1.	C		11.	A
2.	B		12.	B
3.	C		13.	D
4.	C		14.	D
5.	C		15.	C
6.	C		16.	D
7.	A		17.	B
8.	D		18.	C
9.	D		19.	C
10.	B		20.	B

21.	B
22.	C
23.	A
24.	A
25.	A

TEST 2

DIRECTIONS: Each question or incomplete statement is followed by several suggested answers or completions. Select the one that BEST answers the question or completes the statement. *PRINT THE LETTER OF THE CORRECT ANSWER IN THE SPACE AT THE RIGHT.*

1. With regard to typed correspondence received by most offices, which of the following is the GREATEST problem?

      A. Verbosity   B. Illegibility
      C. Improper folding   D. Excessive copies

   1.____

2. Of the following, the GREATEST advantage of flash drives over rewritable CD storage is that they

      A. are portable
      B. are both smaller and lighter
      C. contain more storage space
      D. allow files to be deleted to free space

   2.____

3. Suppose that a large quantity of information is in the files which are located a good distance from your desk. Almost every worker in your office must use these files constantly. Your duties in particular require that you daily refer to about 25 of the same items. They are short, one-page items distributed throughout the files. In this situation, your BEST course would be to

      A. take the items that you use daily from the files and keep them on your desk, inserting *out cards* in their place
      B. go to the files each time you need the information so that the items will be there when other workers need them
      C. make xerox copies of the information you use most frequently and keep them in your desk for ready reference
      D. label the items you use most often with different colored tabs for immediate identification

   3.____

4. Of the following, the MOST important advantage of preparing manuals of office procedures in loose-leaf form is that this form

      A. permits several employees to use different sections simultaneously
      B. facilitates the addition of new material and the removal of obsolete material
      C. is more readily arranged in alphabetical order
      D. reduces the need for cross-references to locate material carried under several headings

   4.____

5. Suppose that you establish a new clerical procedure for the unit you supervise. Your keeping a close check on the time required by your staff to handle the new procedure is WISE mainly because such a check will find out

      A. whether your subordinates know how to handle the new procedure
      B. whether a revision of the unit's work schedule will be necessary as a result of the new procedure
      C. what attitude your employees have toward the new procedure
      D. what alterations in job descriptions will be necessitated by the new procedure

   5.____

6. The numbered statements below relate to the stenographic skill of taking dictation. According to authorities on secretarial practices, which of these are generally recommended guides to development of efficient stenographic skills?

6.____

STATEMENTS

1. A stenographer should date her notebook daily to facilitate locating certain notes at a later time.
2. A stenographer should make corrections of grammatical mistakes while her boss is dictating to her.
3. A stenographer should draw a line through the dictated matter in her notebook after she has transcribed it.
4. A stenographer should write in longhand unfamiliar names and addresses dictated to her.

The CORRECT answer is:

   A. Only Statements 1, 2, and 3 are generally recommended guides.
   B. Only Statements 2, 3, and 4 are generally recommended guides.
   C. Only Statements 1, 3, and 4 are generally recommended guides.
   D. All four statements are generally recommended guides.

7. According to generally recognized rules of filing in an alphabetic filing system, the one of the following names which normally should be filed LAST is

7.____

   A. Department of Education, New York State
   B. F.B.I.
   C. Police Department of New York City
   D. P.S. 81 of New York City

8. Which one of the following forms for the typed name of the dictator in the closing lines of a letter is generally MOST acceptable in the United States?

8.____

   A. (Dr.) James F. Fenton
   B. Dr. James F. Fenton
   C. Mr. James F. Fenton, Ph.D.
   D. James F. Fenton

9. Which of the following is, MOST generally, a rule to be followed when typing a rough draft?

9.____

   A. The copy should be single spaced.
   B. The copy should be triple spaced.
   C. There is no need for including footnotes.
   D. Errors must be neatly corrected.

10. An office assistant needs a synonym.
Of the following, the book which she would find MOST useful is

10.____

   A. a world atlas
   B. BARTLETT'S FAMILIAR QUOTATIONS
   C. a manual of style
   D. a thesaurus

11. Of the following examples of footnotes, the one that is expressed in the MOST generally accepted standard form is: 11.____

    A. Johnson, T.F. (Dr.), <u>English for Everyone</u>, 3rd or 4th edition; New York City Linton Publishing Company, p. 467
    B. Frank Taylor, <u>English for Today</u> (New York: Rayton Publishing Company, 1971), p. 156
    C. Ralph Wilden,<u> English for Tomorrow,</u> Reynolds Publishing Company, England, p. 451
    D. Quinn, David, Yesterday's English (New York: Baldwin Publishing Company, 1972), p. 431

12. Standard procedures are used in offices PRIMARILY because   12.____

    A. an office is a happier place if everyone is doing the tasks in the same manner
    B. particular ways of doing jobs are considered more efficient than other ways
    C. it is good discipline for workers to follow standard procedures approved by the supervisor
    D. supervisors generally don't want workers to be creative in planning their work

13. Assume that an office assistant has the responsibility for compiling, typing, and mailing a preliminary announcement of Spring term course offerings. The announcement will go to approximately 900 currently enrolled students. Assuming that the following equipment is available for use, the MOST EFFECTIVE method for distributing the announcement to all 900 students is to   13.____

    A. e-mail it as a text document using the electronic student mailing list
    B. post the announcement as a PDF document for download on the department website
    C. send it by fax
    D. post the announcement and leave copies in buildings around campus

14. *Justified typing* is a term that refers MOST specifically to typewriting copy   14.____

    A. that has been edited and for which final copy is being prepared
    B. in a form that allows for an even right-hand margin
    C. with a predetermined vertical placement for each alternate line
    D. that has been approved by the supervisor and his superior

15. Which one of the following is the BEST form for the address in a letter?   15.____

    A. Mr. John Jones
       Vice President, The Universal Printing Company
       1220 Fifth Avenue
       New York, 10023 New York
    B. Mr. John Jones, Vice President
       The Universal Printing Company
       1220 Fifth Avenue
       New York, New York 10023
    C. Mr. John Jones, Vice President, The Universal Printing Company
       1220 Fifth Avenue
       New York, New York 10023

D.   Mr. John Jones Vice President,
The Universal Printing Company
1220 Fifth Avenue
New York, 10023 New York

16. Of the following, the CHIEF advantage of the use of window envelopes over ordinary
envelopes is that window envelopes

    A.   eliminate the need for addressing envelopes
    B.   protect the confidential nature of enclosed material
    C.   cost less to buy than ordinary envelopes
    D.   reduce the danger of the address becoming illegible

16.____

17. In the complimentary close of a business letter, the FIRST letter of _____ should be
capitalized.

    A.   all the words   B.   none of the words
    C.   only the first word   D.   only the last word

17.____

18. Assume that one of your duties is to procure needed office supplies from the supply
room. You are permitted to draw supplies every two weeks.
The one of the following which would be the MOST desirable practice for you to follow
in obtaining supplies is to

    A.   obtain a quantity of supplies sufficient to last for several months to make certain
that enough supplies are always on hand
    B.   determine the minimum supply necessary to keep on hand for the various items and
obtain an additional quantity as soon as possible after the supply on hand has been
reduced to this minimum
    C.   review the supplies once a month to determine what items have been exhausted
and obtain an additional quantity as soon as possible
    D.   obtain a supply of an item as soon after it has been exhausted as is possible

18.____

19. Some offices that keep carbon copies of letters use several different colors of carbon
paper for making carbon copies.
Of the following, the CHIEF reason for using different colors of carbon paper is to

    A.   facilitate identification of different types of letters in the files
    B.   relieve the monotony of typing and filing carbon copies
    C.   reduce the costs of preparing carbon copies
    D.   utilize both sides of the carbon paper for typing

19.____

20. Your supervisor asks you to post an online ad for freelance designers interested in
submitting samples for a new company logo. Prospective workers should be proficient in
which of the following software?

    A.   Microsoft Word   B.   Adobe Acrobat Pro
    C.   Adobe Illustrator   D.   Microsoft PowerPoint

20.____

21. Gary Thompson is applying for a position with the firm of Gray and Williams.
Which letter should be filed in top position in the *Application* folder?

    A.   A letter of recommendation written on September 18 by Johnson & Smith
    B.   Williams' letter of October 8 requesting further details regarding Thompson's expe-
rience

21.____

C. Thompson's letter of September 8 making application for a position as sales manager

D. Letter of September 20 from Alfred Jackson recommending Thompson for the job

22. The USUAL arrangement in indexing the names of the First National Bank, Toledo, is   22.____

    A. First National Bank, Toledo, Ohio
    B. Ohio, First National Bank, Toledo
    C. Toledo, First National Bank, Ohio
    D. Ohio, Toledo, First National Bank

23. A single line through typed text indicating that it's incorrect or invalid is known as a(n)   23.____

    A. underline
    B. strikethrough
    C. line font
    D. eraser

24. A typical e-mail with an attachment should contain all of the following for successful transmittal EXCEPT   24.____

    A. recipient's address   B. file attachment
    C. body text   D. description of attachment

25. The subject line in a letter is USUALLY typed a _____ space below the _____.   25.____

    A. single; inside address   B. single; salutation
    C. double; inside address   D. double; salutation

KEY (CORRECT ANSWERS)

1.	A		11.	B
2.	C		12.	B
3.	C		13.	A
4.	B		14.	B
5.	B		15.	B
6.	C		16.	A
7.	D		17.	C
8.	D		18.	B
9.	B		19.	A
10.	D		20.	C

21.	B
22.	A
23.	B
24.	D
25.	D

EXAMINATION SECTION

TEST 1

DIRECTIONS: Each question or incomplete statement is followed by several suggested answers or completions. Select the one that BEST answers the question or completes the statement. *PRINT THE LETTER OF THE CORRECT ANSWER IN THE SPACE AT THE RIGHT.*

1. The one of the following that is MOST advisable to do before transcribing your dictation notes is to
   A. check the syllabification of long words for typing purposes
   B. edit your notes
   C. number the pages of dictation
   D. sort them by the kind of typing format required

1._____

2. As a secretary, the one of the following which is LEAST important in writing a letter under your own signature is
   A. the accuracy of the information
   B. the appropriateness of the language
   C. the reason for the letter
   D. your supervisor's approval of the final copy

2._____

3. In a typed letter, the reference line is used
   A. for identification purposes on typed pages of more than one page
   B. to indicate under what heading the copy of the letter should be filed
   C. to indicate who dictated the letter and who typed it
   D. to make the subject of the letter prominent by typing it a single space below the salutation

3._____

Questions 4-5:

DIRECTIONS: For questions 4 and 5, choose the letter of the sentence that BEST and MOST clearly expresses its meaning.

4.   A. It has always been the practice of this office to effectuate recruitment of prospective employees from other departments.
       B. This office has always made a practice of recruiting prospective employees from other departments.
       C. Recruitment of prospective employees from other departments has always been a practice which has been implemented by this office.
       D. Implementation of the policy of recruitment of prospective employees from other departments has always been a practice of this office.

4._____

5.　　A. These employees are assigned to the level of work evidenced by
　　　　their efforts and skills during the training period.
　　　B. The level of work to which these employees is assigned is
　　　　decided upon on the basis of the efforts and skills evidenced by
　　　　them during the period in which they were trained.
　　　C. Assignment of these employees is made on the basis of the level
　　　　of work their efforts and skills during the training period has
　　　　evidenced.
　　　D. These employees are assigned to a level of work their efforts and
　　　　skills during the training period have evidenced.

5._____

6. An office assistant was asked to mail a duplicated report of 100 pages to
a professor in an out-of-town university. The professor sending the report
dictated a short letter that he wanted to mail with the report.
Of the following, the MOST inexpensive proper means of sending these
two items would be to send the report
　　　A. and the letter first class
　　　B. by parcel post and the letter separately by air mail
　　　C. and the letter by parcel post
　　　D. by parcel post and attach to the package an envelope with first-
　　　　class postage in which is enclosed the letter

6._____

7. Plans are underway to determine the productivity of the typists who work
in a central office. Of the procedures listed, the one generally considered
the MOST accurate for finding out the typists' output is to
　　　A. keep a record of how much typing is done over specified periods
　　　　of time
　　　B. ask each typist how fast she types when she is doing a great deal
　　　　of word processing
　　　C. give each typist a timed test during a specified period
　　　D. ask the supervisor to estimate the typing speed of each
　　　　subordinate

7._____

8. Assume that an executive regularly receives the four types of mail listed
below.
As a general rule, the executive's secretary should arrange the mail from
top to bottom so that the top items are
　　　A. advertisements
　　　B. airmail letters
　　　C. business letters
　　　D. unopened personal letters

8._____

9. An office assistant in transcribing reports and letters from dictation should MOST generally assume that

    9._____

    A. the transcript should be exactly what was dictated so there is little need to check any details
    B. the dictated material is merely an idea of what the dictator wanted to say so changes should be made to improve any part of the dictation
    C. there may be some slight changes, but essentially the transcription is to be a faithful copy of what was dictated
    D. the transcript is merely a very rough draft and should be typed quickly so that the dictator can review it and make changes preliminary to having the final copy typed

10. The one of the following which generally is the CHIEF disadvantage of using office machines in place of human workers in office work is that the machines are

    10._____

    A. slower   B. less accurate
    C. more costly   D. less flexible

11. An office assistant in a New York City college is asked to place a call to a prospective visiting professor in Los Angeles. It is 1 p.m. in New York (EST). The time in Los Angeles is

    11._____

    A. 9 a.m.   B. 10 a.m.   C. 4 p.m.   D. 5 p.m.

12. An office assistant is instructed to send a copy of a report to a professor located in a building across campus. The fastest and most efficient way for this report to reach the professor is by

    12._____

    A. sending a messenger to hand-deliver it to the professor's office
    B. sending it via fax to the main office of the professor's department
    C. e-mailing it to the professor
    D. dictating the contents of the report to the professor over the phone

13. An office assistant is in the process of typing the forms for recommendation for promotion for a member of the faculty who is away for a week. She notes that two books of which he is the author are listed without dates.
Of the following, the procedure she should BEST follow at this point generally is to

    13._____

    A. postpone doing the job until the professor returns to campus the following week
    B. type the material omitting the books
    C. check the professor's office for copies of the books and obtain the correct data
    D. call the professor's wife and ask her when the books were published

14. An office has introduced work standards for all of the employees.
    Of the following, it is MOST likely that use of such standards would tend
    to
    A. make it more difficult to determine numbers of employees needed
    B. lead to a substantial drop in morale among all of the employees
    C. reduce the possibility of planning to meet emergencies
    D. reduce uncertainty about the costs of doing tasks

14._____

15. Of the following clerical errors, the one which probably is LEAST
    important is
    A. adding 543 instead of 548 to a bookkeeping account
    B. putting the wrong code on a data processing card
    C. recording a transaction on the record of Henry Smith instead of on
       the record of Harry Smith
    D. writing John Murpfy instead of John Murphy when addressing an
       envelope

15._____

16. Of the following errors, the one which probably is MOST important is
    A. writing "they're" instead of "their" in an office memo
    B. misplacing a decimal point on a sales invoice
    C. forgetting to write the date on a note for a supervisor
    D. sending an e-mail to a misspelled e-mail address

16._____

17. The chairman of an academic department tells an office assistant that a
    meeting of the faculty is to be held four weeks from the current date.
    Of the following responsibilities, the office assistant is MOST frequently
    held responsible for
    A. planning the agenda of the meeting
    B. presiding over the conduct of the meeting
    C. reserving the meeting room and notifying the members
    D. initiating all formal resolutions

17._____

18. Of the following, a centralized filing system is LEAST suitable for filing
    A. material which is confidential in nature
    B. routine correspondence
    C. periodic reports of the divisions of the department
    D. material used by several divisions of the department

18._____

19. A misplaced record is a lost record.
    Of the following, the MOST valid implication of this statement in regard to
    office work is that
    A. all records in an office should be filed in strict alphabetical order
    B. accuracy in filing is essential
    C. only one method of filing should be used throughout the office
    D. files should be locked when not in use

19._____

20. When typing names or titles on a roll of folder labels, the one of the   20._____
following which is MOST important to do is to type the caption
   A. as it appears on the papers to be placed in the folder
   B. in capital letters
   C. in exact indexing or filing order
   D. so that it appears near the bottom of the folder tab when the label
      is attached

21. A professor at a Boston university asks an office assistant to place a call   21._____
to a fellow professor in San Francisco. The MOST appropriate local time
for the assistant to place the call to the professor in California, given the
time difference, would be
   A. 8:30 a.m.   B. 10:00 a.m.   C. 11:30 a.m.   D. 1:30 p.m.

22. When typing the rough draft of a report, the computer application you   22._____
would use is
   A. Excel   B. Word
   C. PowerPoint   D. Internet Explorer

23. Which of the following is the BEST and most appropriate way to   23._____
proofread and edit a report before submitting it to a supervisor for review?
   A. Scan the report with the program's spell check feature
   B. Proof the report yourself, then ask another office assistant to read
      the report over as well until it is finished
   C. Give the report to another office assistant who is more skilled at
      proofreading
   D. Use the spell checker, then scan the report yourself as many
      times as needed in order to pick up any additional errors

24. The one of the following situations in which it would be MOST justifiable   24._____
for an office to use standard or form paragraphs in its business letters is
when
   A. a large number of similar letters is to be sent
   B. the letters are to be uniform in length and appearance
   C. it is desired to reduce typing errors in correspondence
   D. the office is to carry on a lengthy correspondence with an
      individual

25. Of the following, the MOST important factor in determining whether or not   25._____
an office filing system is effective is that the
   A. information in the files is legible
   B. records in the files are used frequently
   C. information in the files is accurate
   D. records in the files can be located readily

KEY (CORRECT ANSWERS)

1. B	11. B	21. D
2. D	12. C	22. B
3. C	13. C	23. D
4. B	14. D	24. A
5. A	15. D	25. D
6. D	16. B	
7. A	17. C	
8. D	18. A	
9. C	19. B	
10. D	20. C	

TEST 2

DIRECTIONS: Each question or incomplete statement is followed by several suggested answers or completions. Select the one that BEST answers the question or completes the statement. *PRINT THE LETTER OF THE CORRECT ANSWER IN THE SPACE AT THE RIGHT.*

1. For the office assistant whose duties include frequent recording and transcription of minutes of formal meetings, the one of the following reference works generally considered to be MOST useful is
    A. *Robert's Rules of Order*
    B. *Bartlett's Familiar Quotations*
    C. *World Almanac and Book of Facts*
    D. *Conway's Reference*

1._____

2. Of the following statements about the numeric system of filing, the one which is CORRECT is that it
    A. is the least accurate of all methods of filing
    B. eliminates the need for cross-referencing
    C. allows for very limited expansion
    D. requires a separate index

2._____

3. When more than one name or subject is involved in a piece of correspondence to be filed, the office assistant should GENERALLY
    A. prepare a cross-reference sheet
    B. establish a geographical filing system
    C. prepare out-guides
    D. establish a separate index card file for noting such correspondence

3._____

4. A tickler file is MOST generally used for
    A. identification of material contained in a numeric file
    B. maintenance of a current listing of telephone numbers
    C. follow-up of matters requiring future attention
    D. control of records borrowed or otherwise removed from the files

4._____

5. In filing, the name Ms. *Ann Catalana-Moss* should GENERALLY be indexed as
    A. Moss, Catalana, Ann (Ms.)
    B. Catalana-Moss, Ann (Ms.)
    C. Ann Catalana-Moss (Ms.)
    D. Moss-Catalana, Ann (Ms.)

5._____

6. An office assistant has a set of four cards, each of which contains one of
   the following names.
   In alphabetic filing, the FIRST of the cards to be filed is
   A. Ms. Alma John
   B. Mrs. John (Patricia) Edwards
   C. John-Edward School Supplies, Inc.
   D. John H. Edwards

   6._____

7. Generally, of the following, the name to be filed FIRST in an alphabetical
   filing system is
   A. Diane Maestro   B. Diana McElroy
   C. James Mackell   D. James McKell

   7._____

8. After checking several times, you are unable to locate a student record in
   its proper file drawer. The file drawer in question is used constantly by
   many members of the staff.
   In this situation, the NEXT step you should take in locating the missing
   record is to
   A. ask another worker to look through the file drawer
   B. determine if there is another copy of the record filed in a different
      place
   C. find out if the record has been removed by another staff member
   D. wait a day or two and see if the record turns up

   8._____

9. It is MOST important that an enclosure which is to be mailed with a letter
   should be put in an envelope so that
   A. any printing on the enclosure will not be visible through the
      address side of the envelope
   B. it is obvious that there is an enclosure inside the envelope
   C. the enclosure takes up less space than the letter
   D. the person who opens the envelope will pull out both the letter and
      the enclosure

   9._____

10. Suppose that one of the student aides with whom you work suggests a
    change in the filing procedure. He is sure the change will result in
    increased rates of filing among the other employees.
    The one of the following which you should do FIRST is to
    A. ask him to demonstrate his method in order to determine if he files
       more quickly than the other employees
    B. ask your supervisor if you may make a change in the filing
       procedure
    C. ignore the aide's suggestion since he is not a filing expert
    D. tell him to show his method to the other employees and to
       encourage them to use it

    10._____

11. It is generally advisable to leave at least six inches of working space in a   11._____
file drawer. This procedure is MOST useful in
    A. decreasing the number of filing errors
    B. facilitating the sorting of documents and folders
    C. maintaining a regular program of removing inactive records
    D. preventing folders and papers from being torn

12. Assume that a dictator is briefly interrupted because of a telephone call or   12._____
other similar matter (no more than three minutes).
Of the following tasks, the person taking the dictation should NORMALLY
use the time to
    A. re-read notes already recorded
    B. tidy the dictator's desk
    C. check the accuracy of the dictator's desk files
    D. return to her own desk to type the dictated material

13. When typing a preliminary draft of a report, the one of the following which   13._____
you should generally NOT do is
    A. erase typing errors and deletions rather than cross them out
    B. leave plenty of room at the top, bottom and sides of each page
    C. make only the number of copies that you are asked to make
    D. type double or triple space

14. The BEST way for a receptionist to deal with a situation in which she   14._____
must leave her desk for a long time is to
    A. ask someone to take her place while she is away
    B. leave a note or sign on her desk which indicates the time she will
        return
    C. take a chance that no one will arrive while she is gone and leave
        her desk unattended
    D. tell a coworker to ask any visitors that arrive to wait until she
        returns

15. Suppose that two individuals come up to your desk at the same time.   15._____
One of them asks you for the location of the nearest public phone. After
you answer the question, you turn to the second person who asks you the
same question.
The one of the following actions that would be BEST for you to take in this
situation is to
    A. ignore the second person since he obviously overheard your first
        answer
    B. point out that you just answered the same question and quickly
        repeat the information
    C. politely repeat the information to the second individual
    D. tell the second person to follow the first to the public telephone

16. Which of the following names should be filed FIRST in an alphabetical filing system?   16._____
    A. Anthony Aarvedsen   B. William Aaron
    C. Denise Aron   D. A.J. Arrington

17. New material added to a file folder should USUALLY be inserted   17._____
    A. in the order of importance (the most important in front)
    B. in the order of importance (the most important in back)
    C. chronologically (most recent in front)
    D. chronologically (most recent in back)

18. An individual is looking for a name in the White Pages of a telephone directory.   18._____
    Which of the following BEST describes the system of filing found there?
    A. alphabetic   B. sequential
    C. locator   D. index

19. The MAIN purpose of a tickler file is to   19._____
    A. help prevent overlooking matters that require future attention
    B. check on adequacy of past performance
    C. pinpoint responsibility for recurring daily tasks
    D. reduce the volume of material kept in general files

20. Which of the following BEST describes the process of *reconciling* a bank statement?   20._____
    A. Analyzing the nature of the expenditures made by the office during the preceding month
    B. Comparing the statement of the bank with the banking records maintained in the office
    C. Determining the liquidity position by reading the bank statement carefully
    D. Checking the service charges noted on the bank statement

21. From the viewpoint of preserving agency or institutional funds, the LEAST acceptable method for making a payment is a check made out to   21._____
    A. cash   B. a company
    C. an individual   D. a partnership

22. Listed below are four of the steps in the process of preparing correspondence for filing.   22._____
    If they were to be put in logical sequence, the SECOND step would be
    A. preparing cross-reference sheets or cards
    B. coding the correspondence using a classification system
    C. sorting the correspondence in the order to be filed
    D. checking for follow-up action required and preparing a follow-up slip

23. The process of *justifying* typed copy involves laying out the copy so that
    A. each paragraph appears to be approximately the same size
    B. no long words are broken up at the end of a line
    C. the right and left hand margins are even
    D. there is enough room to enter proofreading marks at the end of each line

23._____

24. The MOST important reason for a person in charge of a petty cash fund to obtain receipts for payments is that this practice would tend to
    A. decrease robberies by delivery personnel
    B. eliminate the need to keep a record of petty cash expenditures
    C. prove that the fund has been used properly
    D. provide a record of the need for cash in the daily operations of the office

24._____

25. You should GENERALLY replenish a petty cash fund
    A. at regularly established intervals
    B. each time you withdraw a sum
    C. when the amount of cash gets below a certain specified amount
    D. when the fund is completely empty

25._____

KEY (CORRECT ANSWERS)

1. A	11. D	21. A
2. D	12. A	22. A
3. A	13. A	23. C
4. C	14. A	24. C
5. B	15. C	25. C
6. D	16. B	
7. C	17. C	
8. C	18. A	
9. D	19. A	
10. A	20. B	

EXAMINATION SECTION
TEST 1

DIRECTIONS: Each question or incomplete statement is followed by several suggested
answers or completions. Select the one that BEST answers the question or
completes the statement. *PRINT THE LETTER OF THE CORRECT ANSWER
IN THE SPACE AT THE RIGHT.*

1. In considering a new word processing system for a regional office, which of the following   1._____
would MOST likely be the MOST important consideration in making a decision?

   A. Ease of operation
   B. Friendliness of service technicians
   C. Availability of service technicians
   D. Capacity of the system to meet the unit's word processing needs

2. Your supervisor is out of town for several days and has asked you to act as supervisor in   2._____
his absence. An employee in the unit comes to you and complains that the supervisor
has been dividing the workload unfairly.
Of the following, the MOST appropriate action for you to take is

   A. defend the actions of your supervisor
   B. encourage the employee to file a grievance
   C. listen to the employee attentively
   D. explain to the employee that you have no authority to handle the situation

3. A principal stenographer still on probation is instructed to supervise and coordinate the   3._____
completion of a large word processing project. Her supervisor asks her how long she
thinks the project will take. The principal stenographer gives her supervisor an estimate
that is two days longer than she actually thinks the project will take to complete. The
project is completed two days earlier, and the principal stenographer is congratulated by
her supervisor for her efforts.
In purposely overestimating the time required to complete the project, the principal stenographer showed

   A. *good* judgment because it helped her appear very efficient
   B. *good* judgment because it helps keep unrealistic supervisors from expecting too
much
   C. *poor* judgment because plans and schedules of other components of the project
may have been based on her false estimate
   D. *poor* judgment because she should have used the extra time to further check and,
proofread the work

4. Which of the following would MOST likely be the MOST important in providing support to   4._____
one's supervisor?

   A. Screening annoying phone calls
   B. Reviewing and forwarding articles and publications that may be of interest to your
supervisor
   C. Correctly transmitting instructions from the supervisor to appropriate staff mem-
bers
   D. Reviewing outgoing correspondence for proper grammatical usage and clarity

5. While you are on the telephone answering a question about your agency, a visitor comes to your desk and starts to ask you a question. There is no emergency or urgency in either situation, that of the phone call or that of answering the visitor's question.
In this case, you should

    A. excuse yourself to the person on the telephone and tell the visitor that you will be with him or her as soon as you have finished on the phone
    B. explain to the person on the phone that you have a visitor and must shorten the conversation
    C. continue to talk with the person on the phone while looking up occasionally at the visitor to let him or her know that you know he or she is there
    D. continue to talk with the person on the telephone until you are finished and then let the visitor know that you're sorry to have kept him or her waiting

5.____

6. Your supervisor is out of town on vacation for one week, and asks you to act as supervisor in her absence. The second day she is gone a very important, complex budgetary form, which must be responded to in ten days, arrives in your unit.
Of the following, it would be BEST if you

    A. filled out the form and submitted it as soon as possible
    B. read the form over, did any time-consuming research that might be needed, and then gave the uncompleted form to your supervisor as soon as she returned
    C. asked for help from your supervisor's supervisor in completing the form
    D. tried to contact your supervisor for advice

6.____

7. Of the following, which would MOST likely be of the highest priority?
The typing of

    A. a grant proposal due next week
    B. new addresses onto a mailing list for a future mailing
    C. a payroll form for a new employee that needs to be submitted immediately
    D. a memorandum from the Commissioner to all employees regarding new procedures

7.____

8. Your office is moving to a new location.
Of the following, it would be MOST important to ensure that

    A. others will know your office's new address and phone number
    B. the new office space is comfortable
    C. your supervisor is happy with his or her new office space
    D. the move itself goes smoothly

8.____

9. Of the following, which would generally be considered the LEAST desirable?

    A. Accidentally disconnecting an executive from an important phone call
    B. Ordering the wrong back-up part for a copying machine
    C. Misplacing several hundred dollars worth of personal checks payable to your department
    D. Misplacing a memorandum that needs to be typed

9.____

10. Your supervisor has told you not to let anyone disturb her for the rest of the   10.____
    morning unless absolutely necessary because she has some urgent work to complete.
    The department head telephones and asks to speak to her.
    The BEST course of action for you to take is to

    A. ask the department head if he or she can leave a message
    B. ask your supervisor if she can take the call
    C. tell the department head that your supervisor is out
    D. let your supervisor know that her instructions have put you in a difficult position

11. Which of the following would be MOST likely to contribute to efficiency in the operation of   11.____
    an office?

    A. A new computer system is instituted in an office.
    B. The employees are paid well.
    C. Procedures and practices are studied for any redundant operations.
    D. A supervisor delegates work.

12. You are at work at your desk on a special project when a visitor approaches you. You   12.____
    cannot interrupt your work to take care of this person.
    Of the following, the BEST and MOST courteous way of handling this situation is to

    A. avoid looking up from your work until you are finished with what you are doing
    B. tell the visitor that you will not be able to assist him or her for quite some time
    C. refer the individual to another employee who can take care of him or her right away
    D. chat with the individual while you continue to work

13. Which of the following would MOST likely be of the highest priority?   13.____
    A(n)

    A. annual report due next month
    B. irate member of the public who is standing at your desk
    C. important financial report requested by the Commissioner
    D. memorandum to all employees outlining very important new policy needs to be
       typed and distributed immediately

14. Someone uses *special pull* to obtain the services of your unit at the last minute. You and   14.____
    the four employees you supervise have done everything you could do to provide good
    service, and you feel things have gone very well. The client is not pleased, however, and
    enters your office and begins screaming at you and the other employees present.
    Of the following, it would be BEST if you

    A. ignored the person
    B. tried to calm the person down
    C. asked the person to leave the office
    D. called your supervisor in to help handle the situation

15. Your supervisor is on vacation for two weeks, and you have been asked to fill in for her. 15.____
Your office is very busy, and there is a strict procedure for filling requests. Leslie from Unit X wants something completed immediately. You don't feel this is possible or reasonable, and politely explain why to Leslie. Leslie becomes very angry and says that she will complain to your supervisor about your uncooperative behavior as soon as your supervisor returns.
Of the following, it would be BEST if you

    A. filled Leslie's request
    B. reported Leslie to her supervisor
    C. complained to your supervisor about the situation as soon as she returned
    D. stood by your decision once you determined it was correct

____

KEY (CORRECT ANSWERS)

1. D	6. B	11. C
2. C	7. C	12. C
3. C	8. A	13. B
4. C	9. C	14. B
5. A	10. B	15. D

____

EXAMINATION SECTION
TEST 1

DIRECTIONS: Each question or incomplete statement is followed by several suggested answers or completions. Select the one that BEST answers the question or completes the statement. *PRINT THE LETTER OF THE CORRECT ANSWER IN THE SPACE AT THE RIGHT.*

Questions 1-10.

WORD MEANING

DIRECTIONS: Each question from 1 to 10 contains a word in capitals followed by four suggested meanings of the word. For each question, choose the best meaning. *PRINT THE LETTER OF THE CORRECT ANSWER IN THE SPACE AT THE RIGHT.*

1. ACCURATE   1._____
   A. correct   B. useful   C. afraid   D. careless

2. ALTER   2._____
   A. copy   B. change   C. report   D. agree

3. DOCUMENT   3._____
   A. outline   B. agreement   C. blueprint   D. record

4. INDICATE   4._____
   A. listen   B. show   C. guess   D. try

5. INVENTORY   5._____
   A. custom   B. discovery   C. warning   D. list

6. ISSUE   6._____
   A. annoy   B. use up   C. give out   D. gain

7. NOTIFY   7._____
   A. inform   B. promise   C. approve   D. strengthen

8. ROUTINE   8._____
   A. path   B. mistake   C. habit   D. journey

9. TERMINATE   9._____
   A. rest   B. start   C. deny   D. end

10. TRANSMIT   10._____
    A. put in   B. send   C. stop   D. go across

Questions 11-15.

READING COMPREHENSION

DIRECTIONS: Questions 11 through 15 test how well you understand what you read. It will be necessary for you to read carefully because your answers to these questions should be based ONLY on the information given in the following paragraphs.

The recipient gains an impression of a typewritten letter before he begins to read the message. Pastors which provide for a good first impression include margins and spacing that are visually pleasing, formal parts of the letter which are correctly placed according to the style of the letter, copy which is free of obvious erasures and over-strikes, and transcript that is even and clear. The problem for the typist is that of how to produce that first, positive impression of her work.

There are several general rules which a typist can follow when she wishes to prepare a properly spaced letter on a sheet of letter-head. Ordinarily, the width of a letter should not be less than four inches nor more than six inches. The side margins should also have a desir-able relation to the bottom margin and the space between the letterhead and the body of the letter. Usually the most appealing arrangement is when the side margins are even and the bottom margin is slightly wider than the side margins. In some offices, however, standard line length is used for all business letters, and the secretary then varies the spacing between the date line and the inside address according to the length of the letter.

11. The BEST title for the above paragraphs would be: 11._____

    A. Writing Office Letters
    B. Making Good First Impressions
    C. Judging Well-Typed Letters
    D. Good Placing and Spacing for Office Letters

12. According to the above paragraphs, which of the following might be considered the way   12._____
    in which people very quickly judge the quality of work which has been typed? By

    A. measuring the margins to see if they are correct
    B. looking at the spacing and cleanliness of the typescript
    C. scanning the body of the letter for meaning
    D. reading the date line and address for errors

13. What, according to the above paragraphs, would be definitely UNDESIRABLE as the   13._____
    average line length of a typed letter?

    A. 4"   B. 5"   C. 6"   D. 7"

14. According to the above paragraphs, when the line length is kept standard, the secretary   14._____

    A. does not have to vary the spacing at all since this also is standard
    B. adjusts the spacing between the date line and inside address for different lengths of letters
    C. uses the longest line as a guideline for spacing between the date line and inside address
    D. varies the number of spaces between the lines

15. According to the above paragraphs, side margins are MOST pleasing when they 15.____

    A. are even and somewhat smaller than the bottom margin
    B. are slightly wider than the bottom margin
    C. vary with the length of the letter
    D. are figured independently from the letterhead and the body of the letter

Questions 16-20.

CODING

DIRECTIONS:

Name of Applicant	H	A	N	G	S	B	R	U	K	E
Test Code	c	o	m	p	l	e	x	i	t	y
File Number	0	1	2	3	4	5	6	7	8	9

Assume that each of the above capital letters is the first letter of the name of an Applicant, that the small letter directly beneath each capital letter is the test code for the Applicant, and that the number directly beneath each code letter is the file number for the Applicant.

In each of the following Questions 16 through 20, the test code letters and the file numbers in Columns 2 and 3 should correspond to the capital letters in Column 1. For each question, look at each column carefully and mark your answer as follows:
    If there is an error only in Column 2, mark your
    answer A.
    If there is an error only in Column 3, mark your
    answer B.
    If there is an error in both Columns 2 and 3, mark
    your answer C.
    If both Columns 2 and 3 are correct, mark your
    answer D.

The following sample question is given to help you understand the procedure.

SAMPLE QUESTION

Column 1	Column 2	Column 3
AKEHN	otyci	18902

In Column 2, the final test code letter *i.* should be *m*. Column 3 is correctly coded to Column 1. Since there is an error only in Column 2, the answer is A.

	Column 1	Column 2	Column 3	
16.	NEKKU	mytti	29987	16.____
17.	KRAEB	txyle	86095	17.____
18.	ENAUK	ymoit	92178	18.____
19.	REANA	xeomo	69121	19.____
20.	EKHSE	ytcxy	97049	20.____

Questions 21-30.

ARITHMETICAL REASONING

21. If a secretary answered 28 phone calls and typed the addresses for 112 credit state-   21.____
    ments in one morning, what is the ratio of phone calls answered to credit statements
    typed for that period of time?

    A.   1:4   B.   1:7   C.   2:3   D.   3:5

22. According to a suggested filing system, no more than 10 folders should be filed behind   22.____
    any one file guide and from 15 to 25 file guides should be used in each file drawer for
    easy finding and filing.
    The maximum number of folders that a five-drawer file cabinet can hold to allow easy
    finding and filing is

    A.   550   B.   750   C.   1,100   D.   1,250

23. An employee had a starting salary of $25,804. He received a salary increase at the end   23.____
    of each year, and at the end of the seventh year his salary was $33,476.
    What was his average annual increase in salary over these seven years?

    A. $1,020   B. $1,076   C. $1,096   D. $1,144

24. The 55 typists and 28 senior clerks in a certain city agency were paid a total of   24.____
    $1,943,200 in salaries last year.
    If the average annual salary of a typist was $22,400 the average annual salary of a
    senior clerk was

    A. $25,400   B. $26,600   C. $26,800   D. $27,000

25. A typist has been given a three page report to type. She has finished typing the first two 25.____
    pages. The first page has 283 words, and the second page has 366 words.
    If the total report consists of 954 words, how many words will she have to type on the
    third page of the report?

    A.   202   B.   287   C.   305   D.   313

26. In one day, Clerk A processed 30% more forms than Clerk B, and Clerk C processed li   26.____
    times as many forms as Clerk A. If Clerk B processed 40 forms, how many more forms
    were processed by Clerk C than Clerk B?

    A.   12   B.   13   C.   21   D.   25

27. A clerk who earns a gross salary of $452 every two weeks has the following deductions   27.____
    taken from her paycheck:
    15% for City, State, Federal taxes; 2 1/2% for Social Security; $1.30 for health insur-
    ance; and $6.00 for union dues. The amount of her take-home pay is

    A. $256.20   B. $312.40   C. $331.60   D. $365.60

28. In 2005, a city agency spent $2,000 to buy pencils at a cost of $5.00 a dozen.   28.____
    If the agency used 3/4 of these pencils in 2005 and used the same number of pencils
    in 2006, how many more pencils did it have to buy to have enough pencils for all of
    2006?

    A.   1,200   B.   2,400   C.   3,600   D.   4,800

29. A clerk who worked in Agency X earned the following salaries: $20,140 the first year, $21,000 the second year, and $21,920 the third year. Another clerk who worked in Agency Y for three years earned $21,100 a year for two years and $21,448 the third year. The difference between the average salaries received by both clerks over a three-year period is   29.____

    A. $196   B. $204   C. $348   D. $564

30. An employee who works over 40 hours in any week receives overtime payment for the extra hours at time and one-half (1 1/2 times) his hourly rate of pay. An employee who earns $13.60 an hour works a total of 45 hours during a certain week.
His total pay for that week would be   30.____

    A. $564.40   B. $612.00   C. $646.00   D. $812.00

Questions 31-35.

RELATED INFORMATION

31. To tell a newly-employed clerk to fill a top drawer of a four-drawer cabinet with heavy folders which will be often used and to keep lower drawers only partly filled is   31.____

    A. *good,* because a tall person would have to bend unnecessarily if he had to use a lower drawer
    B. *bad,* because the file cabinet may tip over when the top drawer is opened
    C. *good,* because it is the most easily reachable drawer for the average person
    D. *bad,* because a person bending down at another drawer may accidentally bang his head on the bottom of the drawer when he straightens up

32. If a senior typist or senior clerk has requisitioned a *ream* of paper in order to duplicate a single page office announcement, how many announcements can be printed from the one package of paper?   32.____

    A. 200   B. 500   C. 700   D. 1,000

33. Your supervisor has asked you to locate a telephone number for an attorney named Jones, whose office is located at 311 Broadway, and whose name is not already listed in your files.
The BEST method for finding the number would be for you to   33.____

    A. call the information operator and have her get it for you
    B. look in the alphabetical directory (white pages) under the name Jones at 311 Broadway
    C. refer to the heading Attorney in the yellow pages for the name Jones at 311 Broadway
    D. ask your supervisor who referred her to Mr. Jones, then call that person for the number

34. An example of material that should NOT be sent by first class mail is a   34.____

    A. email copy of a letter   B. post card
    C. business reply card   D. large catalogue

35. In the operations of a government agency, a voucher is ORDINARILY used to   35._____

    A. refer someone to the agency for a position or assignment
    B. certify that an agency's records of financial trans-actions are accurate
    C. order payment from agency funds of a stated amount to an individual
    D. enter a statement of official opinion in the records of the agency

Questions 36-40.

ENGLISH USAGE

DIRECTIONS: Each question from 36 through 40 contains a sentence. Read each sentence carefully to decide whether it is correct. Then, in the space at the right, mark your answer:

    (A) if the sentence is incorrect because of bad grammar or sentence structure

    (B) if the sentence is incorrect because of bad punctuation

    (C) if the sentence is incorrect because of bad capitalization

    (D) if the sentence is correct

Each incorrect sentence has only one type of error. Consider a sentence correct if it has no errors, although there may be other correct ways of saying the same thing.

SAMPLE QUESTION I: One of our clerks were promoted yesterday.

The subject of this sentence is *one,* so the verb should be *was promoted* instead of *were promoted.* Since the sentence is incorrect because of bad grammar, the answer to Sample Question I is (A).

SAMPLE QUESTION II: Between you and me, I would prefer not going there.

Since this sentence is correct, the answer to Sample Question II is (D).

36. The National alliance of Businessmen is trying to persuade private businesses to hire   36._____
youth in the summertime.

37. The supervisor who is on vacation, is in charge of processing vouchers.   37._____

38. The activity of the committee at its conferences is always stimulating.   38._____

39. After checking the addresses again, the letters went to the mailroom.   39._____

40. The director, as well as the employees, are interested in sharing the dividends.   40._____

Questions 41-45.

FILING

DIRECTIONS: Each question from 41 through 45 contains four names. For each question, choose the name that should be FIRST if the four names are to be arranged in alphabeti-cal order in accordance with the Rules for Alphabetical Filing given below. Read these rules carefully. Then, for each question, indicate in the space at the right the letter before the name that should be FIRST in alphabet-ical order.

RULES FOR ALPHABETICAL FILING

Names of People

(1) The names of people are filed in strict alphabetical order, first according to the last name, then according to first name or initial, and finally according to middle name or initial. FOR EXAMPLE: George Allen comes before Edward Bell, and Leonard P. Reston comes before Lucille B. Reston.

(2) When last names are the same, FOR EXAMPLE, A. Green and Agnes Green, the one with the initial comes before the one with the name written out when the first initials are identi-cal.

(3) When first and last names are alike and the middle name is given, FOR EXAMPLE, John David Doe and John Devoe Doe, the names should be filed in the alphabetical order of the middle names.

(4) When first and last names are the same, a name without a middle initial comes before one with a middle name or initial. FOR EXAMPLE, John Doe comes before both John A. Doe and John Alan Doe.

(5) When first and last names are the same, a name with a middle initial comes before one with a middle name beginning with the same initial. FOR EXAMPLE: Jack R. Hertz comes before Jack Richard Hertz.

(6) Prefixes such as De, O', Mac, Mc, and Van are filed as written and are treated as part of the names to which they are connected. FOR EXAMPLE: Robert O'Dea is filed before David Olsen.

(7) Abbreviated names are treated as if they were spelled out. FOR EXAMPLE: Chas. is filed as Charles and Thos. is filed as Thomas.

(8) Titles and designations such as Dr., Mr., and Prof, are disregarded in filing.

Names of Organizations

(1) The names of business organizations are filed according to the order in which each word in the name appears. When an organization name bears the name of a person, it is filed according to the rules for filing names of people as given above. FOR EXAMPLE: William Smith Service Co. comes before Television Distributors, Inc.

(2) Where bureau, board, office, or department appears as the first part of the title of a govern-mental agency, that agency should be filed under the word in the title expressing the chief function of the agency. FOR EXAMPLE: Bureau of the Budget would be filed as if written Budget, (Bureau of the). The Department of Personnel would be filed as if written Person-nel, (Department of).

(3) When the following words are part of an organization, they are disregarded: the, of, and.

(4) When there are numbers in a name, they are treated as if they were spelled out. FOR EXAMPLE: 10th Street Bootery is filed as Tenth Street Bootery.

SAMPLE QUESTION: A.   Jane Earl   (2)
                     B.   James A. Earle   (4)
                     C.   James Earl   (1)
                     D.   J. Earle   (3)

The numbers in parentheses show the proper alphabetical order in which these names should be filed. Since the name that should be filed FIRST is James Earl, the answer to the Sample Question is (C).

41.   A.   Majorca Leather Goods   41._____
      B.   Robert Maiorca and Sons
      C.   Maintenance Management Corp.
      D.   Majestic Carpet Mills

42.   A.   Municipal Telephone Service   42._____
      B.   Municipal Reference Library
      C.   Municipal Credit Union
      D.   Municipal Broadcasting System

43.   A.   Robert B. Pierce   B.   R. Bruce Pierce   43._____
      C.   Ronald Pierce   D.   Robert Bruce Pierce

44.   A.   Four Seasons Sports Club B.   14th. St. Shopping Center   44._____
      C.   Forty Thieves Restaurant D.   42nd St. Theaters

45.   A.   Franco Franceschini   B.   Amos Franchini   45._____
      C.   Sandra Franceschia   D.   Lilie Franchinesca

Questions 46-50.

SPELLING

DIRECTIONS: In each question, one of the words is misspelled. Select the letter of the mis-spelled word. *PRINT THE LETTER OF THE CORRECT ANSWER IN THE SPACE AT THE RIGHT.*

46.   A.   option   B.   extradite   46._____
      C.   comparitive   D.   jealousy

47.   A.   handicaped   B.   assurance   47._____
      C.   sympathy   D.   speech

48.	A.	recommend	B.	carraige
	C.	disapprove	D.	independent

48.____

49.	A.	ingenuity	B.	tenet (opinion)
	C.	uncanny	D.	intrigueing

49.____

50.	A.	arduous	B.	hideous
	C.	iervant	D.	companies

50.____

KEY (CORRECT ANSWERS)

1.	A	11.	D	21.	A	31.	B	41.	C
2.	B	12.	B	22.	D	32.	B	42.	D
3.	D	13.	D	23.	C	33.	C	43.	B
4.	B	14.	B	24.	A	34.	D	44.	D
5.	D	15.	A	25.	C	35.	C	45.	C
6.	C	16.	B	26.	D	36.	C	46.	C
7.	A	17.	C	27.	D	37.	B	47.	A
8.	C	18.	D	28.	B	38.	D	48.	B
9.	D	19.	A	29.	A	39.	A	49.	D
10.	B	20.	C	30.	C	40.	A	50.	C'

EXAMINATION SECTION
TEST 1

DIRECTIONS: Each question or incomplete statement is followed by several suggested answers or completions. Select the one that BEST answers the question or completes the statement. *PRINT THE LETTER OF THE CORRECT ANSWER IN THE SPACE AT THE RIGHT.*

1. A push-button telephone with six buttons, one of which is a *hold* button, is often used when more than one outside line is needed.
    If you are talking on one line of this type of telephone when another call comes in, what is the procedure to follow if you want to answer the second call but keep the first call on the line? Push the

    A. *hold* button at the same time as you push the *pickup* button of the ringing line
    B. *hold* button and then push the *pickup* button of the ringing line
    C. *pickup* button of the ringing line and then push the *hold* button
    D. *pickup* button of the ringing line and push the *hold* button when you return to the original line

1.____

2. Suppose that you are asked to prepare a petty cash statement for March. The original and one copy are to go to the personnel office. One copy is to go to the fiscal office, and another copy is to go to your supervisor. The last copy is for your files.
    In preparing the statement and the copies, how many sheets of copy paper should you use?

    A. 3   B. 4   C. 5   D. 8

2.____

3. Which one of the following is the LEAST important advantage of putting the subject of a letter in the heading to the right of the address?
    It

    A. makes filing of the copy easier
    B. makes more space available in the body of the letter
    C. simplifies distribution of letters
    D. simplifies determination of the subject of the letter

3.____

4. Of the following, the MOST efficient way to put 100 copies of a one-page letter into 9 1/2" x 4 1/8" envelopes for mailing is to fold _____ into an envelope.

    A. each letter and insert it immediately after folding
    B. each letter separately until all 100 are folded; then insert each one
    C. the 100 letters two at a time, then separate them and insert each one
    D. two letters together, slip them apart, and insert each one

4.____

5. When preparing papers for filing, it is NOT desirable to

    A. smooth papers that are wrinkled
    B. use paper clips to keep related papers together in the files
    C. arrange the papers in the order in which they will be filed
    D. mend torn papers with cellophane tape

5.____

6. Of the following, the BEST reason for a clerical unit to have its own duplicating machine is that the unit

    6._____

    A. uses many forms which it must reproduce internally
    B. must make two copies of each piece of incoming mail for a special file
    C. must make seven copies of each piece of outgoing mail
    D. must type 200 envelopes each month for distribution to the same offices

7. Several offices use the same photocopying machine.
If each office must pay its share of the cost of running this machine, the BEST way of determining how much of this cost should be charged to each of these offices is to

    7._____

    A. determine the monthly number of photocopies made by each office
    B. determine the monthly number of originals submitted for photocopying by each office
    C. determine the number of times per day each office uses the photocopy machine
    D. divide the total cost of running the photocopy machine by the total number of offices using the machine

8. Which one of the following would it be BEST to use to indicate that a file folder has been removed from the files for temporary use in another office?
A(n)

    8._____

    A. cross-reference card   B. tickler file marker
    C. aperture card   D. out guide

9. Which one of the following is the MOST important objective of filing?

    9._____

    A. Giving a secretary something to do in her spare time
    B. Making it possible to locate information quickly
    C. Providing a place to store unneeded documents
    D. Keeping extra papers from accumulating on workers' desks

10. If a check has been made out for an incorrect amount, the BEST action for the writer of the check to take is to

    10._____

    A. erase the original amount and enter the correct amount
    B. cross out the original amount with a single line and enter the correct amount above it
    C. black out the original amount so that it cannot be read and enter the correct amount above it
    D. write a new check

11. Which one of the following BEST describes the usual arrangement of a tickler file?

    11._____

    A. Alphabetical   B. Chronological
    C. Numerical   D. Geographical

12. Which one of the following is the LEAST desirable filing practice?

    12._____

    A. Using staples to keep papers together
    B. Filing all material without regard to date
    C. Keeping a record of all materials removed from the files
    D. Writing filing instructions on each paper prior to filing

13. Assume that one of your duties is to keep records of the office supplies used by your unit   13.____
for the purpose of ordering new supplies when the old supplies run out. The information
that will be of MOST help in letting you know when to reorder supplies is the

     A.   quantity issued   B.   quantity received
     C.   quantity on hand   D.   stock number

Questions 14-19.

DIRECTIONS: Questions 14 through 19 consist of sets of names and addresses. In each
question, the name and address in Column II should be an exact copy of the
name and address in Column I. If there is:
a mistake *only* in the name, mark your answer A;
a mistake *only* in the address, mark your answer B;
a mistake in *both* name and address, mark your answer C;
no mistake in *either* name or address, mark your answer D.

SAMPLE QUESTION

Column I	Column II
Michael Filbert	Michael Filbert
456 Reade Street	645 Reade Street
New York, N.Y. 10013	New York, N.Y. 10013

Since there is a mistake only in the address (the street number should be 456
instead of 645), the answer to the sample question is B.

COLUMN I	COLUMN II	
14. Esta Wong 141 West 68 St. New York, N.Y. 10023	Esta Wang 141 West 68 St. New York, N.Y. 10023	14.____
15. Dr. Alberto Grosso 3475 12th Avenue Brooklyn, N.Y. 11218	Dr. Alberto Grosso 3475 12th Avenue Brooklyn, N.Y. 11218	15.____
16. Mrs. Ruth Bortlas 482 Theresa Ct. Far Rockaway, N.Y. 11691	Ms. Ruth Bortlas 482 Theresa Ct. Far Rockaway, N.Y. 11169	16.____
17. Mr. and Mrs. Howard Fox 2301 Sedgwick Ave. Bronx, N.Y. 10468	Mr. and Mrs. Howard Fox 231 Sedgwick Ave. Bronx, N.Y. 10468	17.____
18. Miss Marjorie Black 223 East 23 Street New York, N.Y. 10010	Miss Margorie Black 223 East 23 Street New York, N.Y. 10010	18.____
19. Michelle Herman 806 Valley Rd. Old Tappan, N.J. 07675	Michelle Hermann 806 Valley Dr. Old Tappan, N.J. 07675	19.____

Questions 20-25.

DIRECTIONS: Questions 20 through 25 are to be answered SOLELY on the basis of the information in the following passage.

Basic to every office is the need for proper lighting. Inadequate lighting is a familiar cause of fatigue and serves to create a somewhat dismal atmosphere in the office. One requirement of proper lighting is that it be of an appropriate intensity. Intensity is measured in foot-candles. According to the Illuminating Engineering Society of New York, for casual seeing tasks such as in reception rooms, inactive file rooms, and other service areas, it is recommended that the amount of light be 30 foot-candles. For ordinary seeing tasks such as reading and work in active file rooms and in mail rooms, the recommended lighting is 100 foot-candles. For very difficult seeing tasks such as accounting, transcribing, and business machine use, the recom-mended lighting is 150 foot-candles.

Lighting intensity is only one requirement. Shadows and glare are to be avoided. For example, the larger the proportion of a ceiling filled with lighting units, the more glare-free and comfortable the lighting will be. Natural lighting from windows is not too dependable because on dark wintry days, windows yield little usable light, and on sunny, summer afternoons, the glare from windows may be very distracting. Desks should not face the windows. Finally, the main lighting source ought to be overhead and to the left of the user.

20. According to the above passage, insufficient light in the office may cause   20._____

    A. glare   B. shadows
    C. tiredness   D. distraction

21. Based on the above passage, which of the following must be considered when planning   21._____
     lighting arrangements?
     The

    A. amount of natural light present
    B. amount of work to be done
    C. level of difficulty of work to be done
    D. type of activity to be carried out

22. It can be inferred from the above passage that a well-coordinated lighting scheme is   22._____
     LIKELY to result in

    A. greater employee productivity
    B. elimination of light reflection
    C. lower lighting cost
    D. more use of natural light

23. Of the following, the BEST title for the above passage is   23._____

    A. Characteristics of Light
    B. Light Measurement Devices
    C. Factors to Consider When Planning Lighting Systems
    D. Comfort vs. Cost When Devising Lighting Arrangements

24. According to the above passage, a foot-candle is a measurement of the

    24.____

    A. number of bulbs used
    B. strength of the light
    C. contrast between glare and shadow
    D. proportion of the ceiling filled with lighting units

25. According to the above passage, the number of foot-candles of light that would be needed to copy figures onto a payroll is _____ foot-candles.

    25.____

    A. less than 30   B. 30
    C. 100   D. 150

———

KEY (CORRECT ANSWERS)

1.	B		11.	B
2.	B		12.	B
3.	B		13.	C
4.	A		14.	A
5.	B		15.	D
6.	A		16.	C
7.	A		17.	B
8.	D		18.	A
9.	B		19.	C
10.	D		20.	C

21.	D
22.	A
23.	C
24.	B
25.	D

———

91

TEST 2

DIRECTIONS: Each question or incomplete statement is followed by several suggested answers or completions. Select the one that BEST answers the question or completes the statement. *PRINT THE LETTER OF THE CORRECT ANSWER IN THE SPACE AT THE RIGHT.*

1. Assume that a supervisor has three subordinates who perform clerical tasks. One of the employees retires and is replaced by someone who is transferred from another unit in the agency. The transferred employee tells the supervisor that she has worked as a clerical employee for two years and understands clerical operations quite well. The supervisor then assigns the transferred employee to a desk, tells the employee to begin working, and returns to his own desk.
The supervisor's action in this situation is

   A. *proper;* experienced clerical employees do not require training when they are transferred to new assignments
   B. *improper;* before the supervisor returns to his desk, he should tell the other two subordinates to watch the transferred employee perform the work
   C. *proper;* if the transferred employee makes any mistakes, she will bring them to the supervisor's attention
   D. *improper;* the supervisor should find out what clerical tasks the transferred employee has performed and give her instruction in those which are new or different

1.____

2. Assume that you are falling behind in completing your work assignments and you believe that your workload is too heavy.
Of the following, the BEST course of action for you to take FIRST is to

   A. discuss the problem with your supervisor
   B. decide which of your assignments can be postponed
   C. try to get some of your co-workers to help you out
   D. plan to take some of the work home with you in order to catch up

2.____

3. Suppose that one of the clerks under your supervision is filling in monthly personnel forms. She asks you to explain a particular personnel regulation which is related to various items on the forms. You are not thoroughly familiar with the regulation.
Of the following responses you may make, the one which will gain the MOST respect from the clerk and which is generally the MOST advisable is to

   A. tell the clerk to do the best she can and that you will check her work later
   B. inform the clerk that you are not sure of a correct explanation but suggest a procedure for her to follow
   C. give the clerk a suitable interpretation so that she will think you are familiar with all regulations
   D. tell the clerk that you will have to read the regulation more thoroughly before you can give her an explanation

3.____

4. Charging out records until a specified due date, with prompt follow-up if they are not returned, is a

4.____

A. *good* idea; it may prevent the records from being kept needlessly on someone's desk for long periods of time
B. *good* idea; it will indicate the extent of your authority to other departments
C. *poor* idea; the person borrowing the material may make an error because of the pressure put upon him to return the records
D. *poor* idea; other departments will feel that you do not trust them with the records and they will be resentful

Questions 5-9.

DIRECTIONS: Questions 5 through 9 consist of three lines of code letters and numbers. The numbers on each line should correspond with the code letters on the same line in accordance with the table below.

Code Letter	P	L	I	J	B	O	H	U	C	G
Corresponding Number	0	1	2	3	4	5	6	7	8	9

On some of the lines, an error exists in the coding. Compare the letters and numbers in each question carefully. If you find an error or errors on
    only *one* of the lines in the question, mark your answer A;
    any *two* lines in the question, mark your answer B;
    all *three* lines in the question, mark your answer C;
    none of the lines in the question, mark your answer D.

<u>SAMPLE QUESTION</u>

JHOILCP   3652180
BICLGUP   4286970
UCIBHLJ   5824613

In the above sample, the first line is correct since each code letter listed has the correct corresponding number. On the second line, an error exists because code letter L should have the number 1 instead of the number 6. On the third line, an error exists because the code letter U should have the number 7 instead of the number 5. Since there are errors on two of the three lines, the correct answer is B.

5. BULJCIP   4713920   5._____
    HIGPOUL   6290571
    OCUHJBI   5876342

6. CUBLOIJ   8741023   6._____
    LCLGCLB   1818914
    JPUHIOC   3076158

7. OIJGCBPO   52398405   7._____
    UHPBLIOP   76041250
    CLUIPGPC   81720908

8. BPCOUOJI   40875732   8._____
     UOHCIPLB   75682014
     GLHUUCBJ   92677843

9. HOIOHJLH   65256361   9._____
     IOJJHHBP   25536640
     OJHBJOPI   53642502

Questions 10-13.

DIRECTIONS: Questions 10 through 13 are to be answered SOLELY on the basis of the information given in the following passage.

The mental attitude of the employee toward safety is exceedingly important in preventing accidents. All efforts designed to keep safety on the employee's mind and to keep accident prevention a live subject in the office will help substantially in a safety program. Although it may seem strange, it is common for people to be careless. Therefore, safety education is a continuous process.

Safety rules should be explained, and the reasons for their rigid enforcement should be given to employees. Telling employees to be careful or giving similar general safety warnings and slogans is probably of little value. Employees should be informed of basic safety fundamentals. This can be done through staff meetings, informal suggestions to employees, movies, and safety instruction cards. Safety instruction cards provide the employees with specific suggestions about safety and serve as a series of timely reminders helping to keep safety on the minds of employees. Pictures, posters, and cartoon sketches on bulletin boards that are located in areas continually used by employees arouse the employees' interest in safety. It is usually good to supplement this type of safety promotion with intensive individual follow-up.

10.   The above passage implies that the LEAST effective of the following safety measures is   10._____

    A.   rigid enforcement of safety rules
    B.   getting employees to think in terms of safety
    C.   elimination of unsafe conditions in the office
    D.   telling employees to stay alert at all times

11.   The reason given by the passage for maintaining ongoing safety education is that   11._____

    A.   people are often careless
    B.   office tasks are often dangerous
    C.   the value of safety slogans increases with repetition
    D.   safety rules change frequently

12.   Which one of the following safety aids is MOST likely to be preferred by the passage?   12._____
   A

    A.   cartoon of a man tripping over a carton and yelling, *Keep aisles clear!*
    B.   poster with a large number one and a caption saying, *Safety First*
    C.   photograph of a very neatly arranged office
    D.   large sign with the word *THINK* in capital letters

13. Of the following, the BEST title for the above passage is   13.____

    A. Basic Safety Fundamentals
    B. Enforcing Safety Among Careless Employees
    C. Attitudes Toward Safety
    D. Making Employees Aware of Safety

Questions 14-21.

DIRECTIONS: Questions 14 through 21 are to be answered SOLELY on the basis of the information and the chart given below.

    The following chart shows expenses in five selected categories for a one-year period, expressed as percentages of these same expenses during the previous year. The chart compares two different offices. In Office T (represented by ▨▨▨▨), a cost reduction program has been tested for the past year. The other office, Office Q (represented by ▨▨▨▨), served as a control, in that no special effort was made' to reduce costs during the past year.

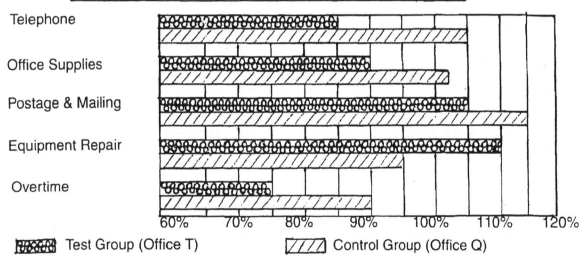

RESULTS OF OFFICE COST REDUCTION PROGRAM

Expenses of Test and Control Groups for 2016
Expressed as Percentages of Same Expenses for 2015

Test Group (Office T)   Control Group (Office Q)

14. In Office T, which category of expense showed the greatest percentage REDUCTION   14.____
from 2015 to 2016?

    A. Telephone   B. Office Supplies
    C. Postage & Mailing   D. Overtime

15. In which expense category did Office T show the BEST results in percentage terms   15.____
when compared to Office Q?

    A. Telephone   B. Office Supplies
    C. Postage & Mailing   D. Overtime

16. According to the above chart, the cost reduction program was LEAST effective for the expense category of   16.____

    A.   Office Supplies   B.   Postage & Mailing
    C.   Equipment Repair   D.   Overtime

17. Office T's telephone costs went down during 2016 by approximately how many percentage points?   17.____

    A.   15   B.   20   C.   85   D.   105

18. Which of the following changes occurred in expenses for Office Supplies in Office Q in the year 2016 as compared with the year 2015?
They   18.____

    A.   increased by more than 100%
    B.   remained the same
    C.   decreased by a few percentage points
    D.   increased by a few percentage points

19. For which of the following expense categories do the results in Office T and the results in Office Q differ MOST NEARLY by 10 percentage points?   19.____

    A.   Telephone   B.   Postage & Mailing
    C.   Equipment Repair   D.   Overtime

20. In which expense category did Office Q's costs show the GREATEST percentage increase in 2016?   20.____

    A.   Telephone   B.   Office Supplies
    C.   Postage & Mailing   D.   Equipment Repair

21. In Office T, by approximately what percentage did overtime expense change during the past year?
It   21.____

    A.   *increased* by 15%   B.   *increased* by 75%
    C.   *decreased* by 10%   D.   *decreased* by 25%

22. In a particular agency, there were 160 accidents in 2007. Of these accidents, 75% were due to unsafe acts and the rest were due to unsafe conditions. In the following year, a special safety program was established. The number of accidents in 2009 due to unsafe acts was reduced to 35% of what it had been in 2007.
How many accidents due to unsafe acts were there in 2009?   22.____

    A.   20   B.   36   C.   42   D.   56

23. At the end of every month, the petty cash fund of Agency A is reimbursed for payments made from the fund during the month. During the month of February, the amounts paid from the fund were entered on receipts as follows: 10 bus fares of 35¢ each and one taxi fare of $3.50.
At the end of the month, the money left in the fund was in the following denominations: 15 one dollar bills, 4 quarters, 10 dimes, and 20 nickels.
If the petty cash fund is reduced by 20% for the following month, how much money will there be available in the petty cash fund for March?   23.____

    A. $11.00   B. $20.00   C. $21.50   D. $25.00

24. The one of the following records which it would be MOST advisable to keep in alphabetical order is a   24.____

    A.   continuous listing of phone messages, including time and caller, for your supervisor
    B.   listing of individuals currently employed by your agency in a particular title
    C.   record of purchases paid for by the petty cash fund
    D.   dated record of employees who have borrowed material from the files in your office

25. Assume that you have been asked to copy by hand a column of numbers with two decimal places from one record to another. Each number consists of three, four, and five digits.
In order to copy them quickly and accurately, you should copy   25.____

    A.   each number exactly, making sure that the column of digits farthest to the right is in a straight line and all other columns are lined up
    B.   the column of digits farthest to the right and then copy the next column of digits moving from right to left
    C.   the column of digits farthest to the left and then copy the next column of digits moving from left to right
    D.   the digits to the right of each decimal point and then copy the digits to the left of each decimal point

_____

KEY (CORRECT ANSWERS)

1.	D		11.	A
2.	A		12.	A
3.	D		13.	D
4.	A		14.	D
5.	A		15.	A
6.	C		16.	C
7.	D		17.	A
8.	B		18.	D
9.	C		19.	B
10.	D		20.	C

21.	D
22.	C
23.	B
24.	B
25.	A

_____

VERBAL & CLERICAL ABILITIES
EXAMINATION SECTION
TEST 1

DIRECTIONS: Read each question carefully. Select the best answer and write the letter in the answer space at the right.

1. PREVIOUS means most nearly
   A. abandoned
   B. timely
   C. former
   D. successive
   E. younger

1._____

2. CONSENSUS means most nearly
   A. accord
   B. abridgment
   C. presumption
   D. quota
   E. exception

2._____

3. LACONIC means most nearly
   A. slothful
   B. concise
   C. punctual
   D. melancholy
   E. indifferent

3._____

4. TRENCHANT means most nearly
   A. urgent
   B. witty
   C. decisive
   D. sharp
   E. merciless

4._____

5. MANDATORY means most nearly
   A. basic
   B. obligatory
   C. discretionary
   D. discriminatory
   E. advisory

5._____

6. OPTION means most nearly
   A. use
   B. choice
   C. value
   D. blame
   E. rule

6._____

7. INNATE means most nearly
    A. eternal
    B. well-developed
    C. native
    D. prospective
    E. understandable

7._____

8. To CONFINE means most nearly to
    A. restrict
    B. hide
    C. eliminate
    D. punish
    E. ruin

8._____

9. A small crane was used to *raise* the heavy parts.
   Raise means most nearly
    A. drag
    B. unload
    C. deliver
    D. lift
    E. guide

9._____

10. The reports were *consolidated* by the secretary.
   Consolidated means most nearly
    A. combined
    B. concluded
    C. distributed
    D. protected
    E. weighed

10._____

11. CROWD is related to PERSONS as FLEET is related to
    A. guns
    B. officers
    C. navy
    D. expedition
    E. ships

11._____

12. SPEEDOMETER is related to POINTER as WATCH is related to
    A. case
    B. hands
    C. dial
    D. numerals
    E. band

12._____

13. PLUMBER is related to WRENCH as PAINTER is related to
    A. brush
    B. pipe
    C. shop
    D. hammer
    E. painting

13._____

14. BODY is related to FOOD as ENGINE is related to   14._____
  A. wheels
  B. smoke
  C. motion
  D. fuel
  E. conductor

15. ABUNDANT is related to CHEAP as SCARCE is related to 15._____
  A. ample
  B. inexpensive
  C. costly
  D. unobtainable
  E. frugal

Reading

16. "One type of advertising on which it is difficult to calculate the return is the radio 16._____
program, offered by so many industries today. The chief return of radio
advertising is goodwill, which industries consider so valuable that they spend
vast sums of money to obtain it."

The quotation BEST supports the statement that radio advertising by industries
  A. is more expensive than other advertising
  B. has its chief value in creating goodwill
  C. is used by all large industries
  D. is of little value
  E. is the most valuable form of advertising

17. "Just as the procedure of a collection department must be clear-cut and definite, 17._____
the steps being taken with the sureness of a skilled chess player, so the various
paragraphs of a collection letter must show clear organization, giving evidence of
a mind that, from the beginning, has had a specific end in view."

The quotation BEST supports the statement that a collection letter should always
  A. show a spirit of sportsmanship
  B. be divided into several paragraphs
  C. express confidence in the debtor
  D. be brief, but courteous
  E. be carefully planned

18. "One of the primary steps in the development of management in any enterprise is proper organization. After the business has been conceived and the broad policies that are to be pursued have been established, before any operating methods may be devised, at least a skeleton organization must be developed."

18._____

The quotation BEST supports the statement that, in industry, some kind of organization is necessary in order that
    A. the type of enterprise may be decided upon
    B. policies may be established
    C. routine work may be planned
    D. capital may be invested
    E. a manager may be selected

19. "The division of labor into the categories of physical and mental labor is not strictly accurate. The labor of even the most unskilled workman calls for the exercise of certain mental qualities, like attention, memory, and prudence; and on the other hand, the intellectual effort of the great captains of industry is associated with a certain amount of waste of tissue."

19._____

The quotation BEST supports the statement that
    A. There is no real distinction between physical and mental labor.
    B. Manual labor does not call for so great a waste of tissue as intellectual effort does.
    C. The exercise of mental qualities remains the most important feature of labor.
    D. Physical and mental labor require use of the same mental qualities.
    E. The difference between various forms of labor is one of degree.

20. "Proper supervision of play involves a recognition of the fact that a happy childhood through play is essential to a child's normal growth and personal development. Self-discipline and right conduct are natural results of a situation in which a child engages in activities of absorbing interest under wise guidance."

20._____

The quotation BEST supports the statement that the proper supervision of play
    A. is of greater benefit to some children than to others
    B. has as its chief purpose training for self-discipline
    C. helps a child to obtain satisfactory results from his recreation
    D. is less essential as a child becomes more absorbed in his play
    E. provides for the natural development of differences in personalities

21. "Alertness and attentiveness are qualities essential for success as a receptionist. The work the receptionist performs often takes careful attention under conditions of stress."

21._____

The quotation BEST supports the statement that a receptionist
    A. always works under great strain
    B. cannot be successful unless she memorizes many extensions
    C. must be trained before she can render good service
    D. must be able to work under difficulties
    E. performs more difficult work than do clerical office workers

22. "Probably few people realize, as they drive on a concrete road, that steel is used   22._____
to keep the surface flat and even, in spite of the weight of busses and trucks.
Steel bars, deeply imbedded in the concrete, provide sinews to take the stresses
so that they cannot crack the slab or make it wavy."

The quotation BEST supports the statement that a concrete road
    A. is expensive to build
    B. usually cracks under heavy weights
    C. is used exclusively for heavy traffic
    D. is reinforced with other material

23. "Whenever two groups of people whose interests at the moment conflict meet to   23._____
discuss a solution of that conflict, there is laid the basis for an interchange of
facts and ideas which increases the total range of knowledge of both parties and
tends to break down the barrier which their restricted field of information has
helped to create."

The quotation BEST supports the statement that conflicts between two parties
may be brought closer to a settlement through
    A. frank acknowledgment of error
    B. the exchange of accusations
    C. gaining a wider knowledge of facts
    D. submitting the dispute to an impartial judge
    E. limiting discussion to plans acceptable to both groups

24. "What constitutes skill in any line of work is not always easy to determine;   24._____
economy of time must be carefully distinguished from economy of energy, as the
quickest method may require the greatest expenditure of muscular effort, and
may not be essential or at all desirable."

The quotation BEST supports the statement that
    A. energy and time cannot both be conserved in the performing of a single
       task
    B. the most efficiently executed task is not always the one done in the shortest
       time
    C. if a task requires muscular energy, it is not being performed economically
    D. skill in performing a task should not be acquired at the expense of time
    E. a task is well done when it is performed in the shortest time

25. "The secretarial profession is a very old one and has increased in importance   25._____
with the passage of time. In modern times, the vast expansion of business and
industry has greatly increased the need and opportunities for secretaries, and for
the first time in history their number has become large."

The quotation BEST supports the statement that the secretarial profession
    A. is older than business and industry
    B. did not exist in ancient times
    C. has greatly increased in size
    D. demands higher training than it did formerly
    E. is not in high enough demand

26. "It is difficult to distinguish between bookkeeping and accounting. In attempts to do so, bookkeeping is called the art, and accounting the science, of recording business transactions. Bookkeeping gives the history of the business in a systematic manner; and accounting classifies, analyzes, and interprets the facts thus recorded."

    The quotation BEST supports the statement that
    A. accounting is less systematic than bookkeeping
    B. accounting and bookkeeping are closely related
    C. bookkeeping and accounting cannot be distinguished from one another
    D. bookkeeping has been superseded by accounting
    E. bookkeeping is more practical than accounting

26._____

Spelling. Find which choice is spelled correctly and mark the letter in the space at the right.

27. A. athalete
    B. athlete
    C. athelete
    D. none of the above

27._____

28. A. predesessor
    B. predecesar
    C. predecesser
    D. none of the above

28._____

29. A. occasion
    B. occasion
    C. ocassion
    D. none of the above

29._____

30. A. Mobile, Ala.
    B. Brocton, Mass.
    C. Yeork, Pa.
    D. Sou Falls, S. Dak.
    E. none of the above

30._____

31. A. Brookelin, N.Y.
    B. Alambra, Calif.
    C. Attlanta, Ga.
    D. Joplinn, Mo.
    E. none of the above

31._____

Grammar. Decide which sentence is preferable with respect to grammar and usage suitable for a formal letter or report and mark the letter in the space at the right.

32. A. They do not ordinarily present these kind of reports in detail like this.
    B. Reports like this is not generally given in such great detail.
    C. A report of this kind is not hardly ever given in such detail as this one.
    D. This report is more detailed than what such reports ordinarily are.
    E. A report of this kind is not ordinarily presented in such detail as this one.

32._____

33. A. No other city anywheres in the State has grown so fast as this city.
    B. This city has grown more rapidly than any other city in the State.
    C. No other city in the State has grown as fast or faster than this city.
    D. The growth of this city has been more rapid than any other city in the State.
    E. This city has grown the fastest of all the others in the State.

33._____

34. A. The manager told Mr. Jones and I that we were expected to attend the meeting.
    B. Mr. Jones and I were told by the manager that is was necessary for both of us to have attended the meeting.
    C. In his talk with Mr. Jones and I, the manager explained that our attendance at the meeting was expected.
    D. The manager said that he expected Mr. Jones and me to attend the meeting.
    E. The manager explained to Mr. Jones and myself that it was necessary for us to be present at the meeting.

34._____

35. A. Neither the editor nor his assistant will approve that type of report.
    B. That kind of a report is not acceptable to either the editor or his assistant.
    C. A report of that kind is acceptable to neither the editor or his assistant.
    D. Both the editor and his assistant are sort of unwilling to approve a report like that.
    E. Neither the editor nor his assistant are willing to approve that type of report.

35._____

36. A. I haven't no report on your call yet.
    B. I had ought to receive a report on your call soon.
    C. Can I ring you when I have a report on your call?
    D. Do you want for me to ring as soon as I receive a report on your call?
    E. I do not have any report on your call yet.

36._____

37. A. Our activities this month have been as interesting, if not more interesting than those of any other month this year.
    B. Our activities this year have seldom ever been as interesting as they have been this month.
    C. Our activities this month have been more interesting than those of any other month this year.
    D. Our activities this month have been more interesting, or at least as interesting as those of any month this year.
    E. This month's activities have been more interesting than any previous month during the year.

37._____

38. A. If properly addressed, the letter will reach my mother and I.
    B. The letter had been addressed to myself and my mother.
    C. I believe the letter was addressed to either my mother or I.
    D. My mother's name, as well as mine, was on the letter.
    E. The letter will get to my mother and myself if properly addressed.

38._____

39. A. Most all these statements have been supported by persons who are reliable
       and can be depended upon.
    B. The persons which have guaranteed these statements are reliable.
    C. Reliable persons guarantee the facts with regards to the truth of these
       statements.
    D. These statements can be depended on, for their truth has been guaranteed by
       reliable persons.
    E. The persons who guarantee these statements are very much reliable.

39._____

40. A. Brown's & Company employees have recently received increases in salary.
    B. Brown & Company recently increased the salaries of all its employees.
    C. Recently Brown & Company has increased their employees' salaries.
    D. Brown & Company have recently increased the salaries of all its employees.
    E. Brown & Company employees have all been increased in salary.

40._____

KEY (CORRECT ANSWERS)

1.	C	16.	B	31.	E
2.	A	17.	E	32.	E
3.	B	18.	C	33.	B
4.	D	19.	E	34.	D
5.	B	20.	C	35.	A
6.	B	21.	D	36.	E
7.	C	22.	D	37.	C
8.	A	23.	C	38.	D
9.	D	24.	B	39.	D
10.	A	25.	C	40.	B
11.	E	26.	B		
12.	B	27.	B		
13.	A	28.	D		
14.	D	29.	B		
15.	C	30.	A		

TEST 2

Questions 1-4.

DIRECTIONS: Below are underlined names, followed by alphabetical names. The spaces between names are lettered A, B, C, D, and E. Decide in which space the underlined name belongs and write the letter in the answer space at right.

1. <u>Kessler, Neilson</u>   1._____

    A)_____

       Kessel, Oscar

    B)_____

       Kessinger, D.J.

    C)_____

       Kessler, Karl

    D)_____

       Kessner, Lewis

    E)_____

2. <u>Jones, Jane</u>   2._____

    A)_____

       Goodyear, G.L.

    B)_____

       Haddon, Harry

    C)_____

       Jackson, Mary

    D)_____

       Jenkins, William

    E)_____

3. <u>Olsen, C.C.</u>   3._____

    A)_____

       Olsen, C.A.

    B)_____

       Olsen, C.D.

    C)_____

       Olsen, Charles

    D)_____

       Olsen, Christopher

    E)_____

4. <u>DeMattia, Jessica</u>   4._____

    A)_____

       DeLong, Jesse

    B)_____

       DeMatteo, Jessie

    C)_____

       Derby, Jessie S.

    D)_____

       DeShazo, L.M.

    E)_____

Question 5.

DIRECTIONS: Following are a group of four related sentences, which may or may
not be in logical order. Following the sentences are five suggested
sequences, lettered A, B, C, D, and E, from which you are to select
the one that indicates the best arrangement of sentences. Indicate
your choice of letters in the space at right.

5. (1) It must be comparatively scarce, and it should have a stable value.   5._____
   (2) In order to serve satisfactorily as money, a substance must have certain
      qualities.
   (3) It should also be durable, and its value should be high in proportion to its
      bulk.
   (4) Gold and silver have been widely used for money because they possess
      these qualities to a greater extent than do other commodities.

    A. 2-4-1-3
    B. 2-3-1-4
    C. 2-1-4-3
    D. 2-1-3-4
    E. 2-4-3-1

Question 6.

DIRECTIONS: Following is a sentence with an underlined word that is spelled as it
is pronounced. Write the correct spelling of the word in the blank.
Then decide which one of the suggested answers, A, B, C, or D, is
the correct answer to the question, and write the letter in the space
at right.

6. The new treasurer uses the same system that his pred-eh-sess´-urr did.   6._____
   In the correct spelling, _____, what is the tenth
   letter?
    A. s
    B. e
    C. o
    D. none of the above

Questions 7-11.

DIRECTIONS: In each line there are three names or numbers that are much alike. Compare the three names or numbers and decide which ones are exactly alike. Fill in the letter
A. if ALL THREE names or number are exactly ALIKE
B. if only the FIRST and SECOND names or numbers are exactly ALIKE
C. if only the FIRST and THIRD names or numbers are exactly ALIKE
D. if only the SECOND and THIRD names or numbers are exactly ALIKE
E. if ALL THREE names or numbers are DIFFERENT

7. Davis Hazen	David Hozen	David Hazen	7._____
8. Lois Appel	Lois Appel	Lois Apfel	8._____
9. June Allan	Jane Allan	Jane Allan	9._____
10. 10235	10235	10235	10._____
11. 32614	32164	32614	11._____

Questions 12-22.

DIRECTIONS: Compute the answer and compare it with suggested answers. Mark the letter in the space at right.

12. Add: 12._____

```
  963
  257
+416
```

A. 1,516
B. 1,526
C. 1,636
D. 1,726
E. none of the above

13. Add: 13._____

    22
  +33

    A. 44
    B. 45
    C. 54
    D. 55
    E. none of the above

14. Add: 14._____

  $5.2 + .96 + 47.0 =$

    A. 19.5
    B. 48.48
    C. 53.16
    D. 42.98
    E. none of the above

15. Subtract: 15._____

    24
   - 3

    A. 20
    B. 21
    C. 27
    D. 29
    E. none of the above

16. Subtract: 16._____

    33
   -8

    A. 25
    B. 26
    C. 35
    D. 36
    E. none of the above

17. Subtract: 17._____

    219
    -110

    A. 99
    B. 109
    C. 199
    D. 189
    E. none of the above

18. Multiply: 18._____

    25
    X5

    A. 100
    B. 115
    C. 125
    D. 135
    E. none of the above

19. Multiply: 19._____

    45
    X5

    A. 200
    B. 215
    C. 225
    D. 235
    E. none of the above

20. 47% of 538 =   20._____

    A. 11.45
    B. 252.86
    C. 285.14
    D. 265.66
    E. none of the above

21. Divide: 21._____

    $6\overline{)126}$

    A. 20
    B. 22
    C. 24
    D. 26
    E. none of the above

22. Divide:

22._____

$$40\,\overline{)\,1{,}208}$$

   A. 3
   B. 30
   C. 33
   D. 40
   E. none of the above

Questions 23-32.

DIRECTIONS: For each question, find which one of the suggested answers contains numbers and letters all of which appear in that question. These numbers and letters may be in any order in the question, but all four must appear. If neither A, B, C, nor D fits, mark E for that question. Mark your answer in the space at right.

23. 8 N K 9 G T 4 6   23._____

24. T 9 7 Z 6 L 3 K   24._____

25. Z 7 G K 3 9 8 N   25._____

26. 3 K 9 4 6 G Z L   26._____

27. Z N 7 3 8 K T 9   27._____

Suggested Answers for Questions 23-27:
A = 7, 9, G, K
B = 8, 9, T, Z
C = 6, 7, K, Z
D = 6, 8, G, T
E = none of the above

113

28. 2 3 P 6 V Z 4 L   28._____

29. T 7 4 3 P Z 9 G   29._____

30. 6 N G Z 3 9 P 7   30._____

31. 9 6 P 4 N G Z 2   31._____

32. 4 9 7 T L P 3 V   32._____

Suggested Answers for Questions 28-32:
A = 3, 6, G, P
B = 3, 7, P, V
C = 4, 6, V, Z
D = 4, 7, G, Z
E = none of the above

Questions 33-34.

DIRECTIONS: Consider the figures below to be correct figures.

The figures below are incorrect because the slope of one of the lines differs from the slope in one of the similar correct figures.

The following questions show four correct figures and one incorrect figure. Select the letter of the incorrect figure and mark the letter in the space at right.

33.

   A   B   C   D   E

33._____

34.

___ ___ ___ ___ ___
___ ___ ___ ___ ___
 A   B   C   D   E

34._____

Questions 35-48

DIRECTIONS: On the left is a series of numbers or letters which follow some definite order. Pick the answer that follows the order and write the letter of your choice in the space at right.

35. x c x d x e x

   A. f x
   B. f g
   C. x f
   D. e f
   E. x g

35._____

36. a b d c e f h

   A. c h
   B. i g
   C. g i
   D. k l
   E. i h

36._____

37. 15 14 13 12 11 10 9

   A. 2 1
   B. 17 16
   C. 8 9
   D. 8 7
   E. 9 8

37._____

38. 20 20 21 21 22 22 23

   A. 23 23
   B. 23 24
   C. 19 19
   D. 22 23
   E. 21 22

38._____

39. 17 3 17 4 17 5 17

39._____

    A. 6 17
    B. 6 7
    C. 17 6
    D. 5 6
    E. 17 7

40. 1 2 4 5 7 8 10

40._____

    A. 11 12
    B. 12 14
    C. 10 13
    D. 12 13
    E. 11 13

41. 21 21 20 20 19 19 18

41._____

    A. 18 18
    B. 18 17
    C. 17 18
    D. 17 17
    E. 18 19

42. 1 20 3 19 5 18 7

42._____

    A. 8 9
    B. 8 17
    C. 17 10
    D. 17 9
    E. 9 18

43. 30 2 28 4 26 6 24

43._____

    A. 23 9
    B. 26 8
    C. 8 9
    D. 26 22
    E. 8 22

44. 5 6 20 7 8 19 9

44._____

    A. 10 18
    B. 18 17
    C. 10 17
    D. 18 19
    E. 10 11

45. 9 10 1 11 12 2 13   45._____

    A. 2 14
    B. 3 14
    C. 14 3
    D. 14 15
    E. 14 1

46. 4 6 9 11 14 16 19   46._____

    A. 21 24
    B. 22 25
    C. 20 22
    D. 21 23
    E. 22 24

47. 8 8 1 10 10 3 12   47._____

    A. 13 13
    B. 12 5
    C. 12 4
    D. 13 5
    E. 4 12

48. 20 21 23 24 27 28 32 33 38 39   48._____

    A. 45 46
    B. 45 54
    C. 44 45
    D. 44 49
    E. 40 46

Questions 49-53.

DIRECTIONS: Each of the following questions consists of two sets of symbols. Find the one rule that (a) explains the similarity of the symbols within each set, and (b) also explains the difference between the sets. Among the five suggested answers, find the symbol that can best be substituted for the question mark in the second set. In all these questions you will find details that have nothing to do with the principle of the question: to find the similarity between the symbols within a set and the difference between the sets. Mark the letter of your answer choice in the space at right.

49.   SET 1   SET 2   49._____

50. SET 1   SET 2   50._____

51. SET 1   SET 2   51._____

52. SET 1   SET 2   52._____

53. SET 1   SET 2   53._____

Questions 54-56.

DIRECTIONS: Following are word problems. Mark the letter of the answer you choose in the space at right.

54. The safety rules of Factory X require that the operator of a certain machine take a rest period of 15 minutes after working 2 consecutive hours. If the workday consists of 3 3/4 hours in the morning, 30 minutes for lunch, and 4 1/4 hours in the afternoon, a job that requires 29 machine hours to complete will take the operator of this machine   54._____

A. less than 3 days
B. between 3 and 3 1/2 days
C. 3 1/2 days
D. between 3 1/2 and 4 days
E. 4 days or longer

55. The weight of water is 62.4 pounds per cubic foot. What is the weight of the water that fills a rectangular container 6 inches by 6 inches by 1 foot?   55._____

A. 1.7 pounds
B. 10.4 pounds
C. 31.2 pounds
D. 249.6 pounds
E. none of the above

56. The inventor of a machine which operates by solar heat claims that it accumulates heat in the daytime at the rate of 10 units an hour on sunny days and 3 units an hour on cloudy days. During rain there is no accumulation of heat. In July there were 22 hours of daylight rain and 42 hours of cloudy daylight. Assuming on the average 13 hours of daylight per day in July, how many units should the machine have accumulated that month?

56._____

    A. 339
    B. 403
    C. 3,516
    D. 3,810
    E. none of the above

Questions 57-60

DIRECTIONS: Refer to the tables and charts to answer the following questions, and mark the letter of the correct answer in the space at right.

CONSUMPTION OF FUELS FOR PRODUCTION OF ELECTRIC ENERGY
1998-2003

	1998	1999	2000	2001	2002	2003
Bituminous and lignite coal (thousands short tons)	165,794	173,882	179,612	190,941	200,193	223,162
Anthracite coal (thousands short tons)	2,629	2,751	2,509	2,297	2,139	2,239
Fuel oil (thousands of barrels)	88,263	85,340	85,736	85,768	93,314	101,162
Gas (millions of cubic feet)	1,628,509	1,724,762	1,825,117	1,955,974	2,144,473	2,321,889

57. In which year did the greatest number of kinds of fuel show an increase in consumption over that of the preceding year?

57._____

    A. 1999
    B. 2000
    C. 2001
    D. 2002
    E. 2003

58. The total amount of coal consumed in the production of electric energy in 2003   58._____
was approximately what percent of that consumed in 1998?

    A. 57%
    B. 75%
    C. 134%
    D. 150%
    E. 168%

POPULATION MOVEMENT TO AND FROM COUNTY X
1982 TO 2003

MOVING TO COUNTY ------------
MOVING FROM COUNTY —————

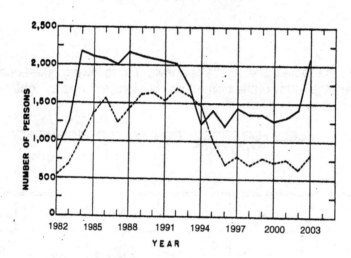

59. The graph above indicates that, with respect to County X, migratory activities   59._____
during the period from 1982 to 2003 tended mostly to result in

    A. population gains
    B. population losses
    C. gradual stabilization of population
    D. irregular fluctuations in population without consistent direction
    E. cycles of alternating losses and gains in population which tended to
       balance each other

60. The ratio of the number of persons who left to the number who entered County X   60._____
in 2003 is approximately

    A. 12 to 7
    B. 7 to 12
    C. 2 to 5
    D. 5 to 2
    E. 5 to 3

KEY (CORRECT ANSWERS)

1.	D	16.	A	31.	E	46.	A
2.	E	17.	B	32.	B	47.	B
3.	B	18.	C	33.	A	48.	A
4.	C	19.	C	34.	B	49.	E
5.	D	20.	B	35.	A	50.	D
6.	C	21.	E	36.	C	51.	B
7.	E	22.	E	37.	D	52.	E
8.	B	23.	D	38.	B	53.	B
9.	D	24.	C	39.	A	54.	D
10.	A	25.	A	40.	E	55.	E
11.	C	26.	E	41.	B	56.	C
12.	C	27.	B	42.	D	57.	E
13.	D	28.	C	43.	E	58.	C
14.	C	29.	D	44.	A	59.	B
15.	B	30.	A	45.	C	60.	D

CLERICAL ABILITIES TEST

EXAMINATION SECTION
TEST 1

DIRECTIONS: Each question or incomplete statement is followed by several suggested answers or completions. Select the one that *BEST* answers the question or completes the statement. *PRINT THE LETTER OF THE CORRECT ANSWER IN THE SPACE AT THE RIGHT.*

Questions 1-10.

DIRECTIONS: Questions 1 through 10 consist of lines of names, dates and numbers. For each question, you are to choose the option (A, B, C, or D) in Column II which *EXACTLY* matches the information in Column I. *PRINT THE LETTER OF THE CORRECT ANSWER IN THE SPACE AT THE RIGHT.*

SAMPLE QUESTION

Column I	Column II
Schneider 11/16/75 581932	A. Schneider 11/16/75 518932
	B. Schneider 11/16/75 581932
	C. Schnieder 11/16/75 581932
	D. Shnieder 11/16/75 518932

The correct answer is B. Only option B shows the name, date and number exactly as they are in Column I. Option A has a mistake in the number. Option C has a mistake in the name. Option D has a mistake in the name and in the number. Now answer Questions 1 through 10 in the same manner.

Column I   Column II

1. Johnston 12/26/74 659251
  A. Johnson 12/23/74 659251   1.____
  B. Johston 12/26/74 659251
  C. Johnston 12/26/74 695251
  D. Johnston 12/26/74 659251

2. Allison 1/26/75 9939256
  A. Allison 1/26/75 9939256   2.____
  B. Alisson 1/26/75 9939256
  C. Allison 1/26/76 9399256
  D. Allison 1/26/75 9993256

3. Farrell 2/12/75 361251
  A. Farell 2/21/75 361251   3.____
  B. Farrell 2/12/75 361251
  C. Farrell 2/21/75 361251
  D. Farrell 2/12/75 361151

4. Guerrero 4/28/72 105689
  A. Guererro 4/28/72 105689   4.____
  B. Guerrero 4/28/72 105986
  C. Guerrero 4/28/72 105869
  D. Guerrero 4/28/72 105689

5. McDonnell 6/05/73 478215

    A. McDonnell 6/15/73 478215
    B. McDonnell 6/05/73 478215
    C. McDonnell 6/05/73 472815
    D. MacDonell 6/05/73 478215

5.____

6. Shepard 3/31/71 075421

    A. Sheperd 3/31/71 075421
    B. Shepard 3/13/71 075421
    C. Shepard 3/31/71 075421
    D. Shepard 3/13/71 075241

6.____

7. Russell 4/01/69 031429

    A. Russell 4/01/69 031429
    B. Russell 4/10/69 034129
    C. Russell 4/10/69 031429
    D. Russell 4/01/69 034129

7.____

8. Phillips 10/16/68 961042

    A. Philipps 10/16/68 961042
    B. Phillips 10/16/68 960142
    C. Phillips 10/16/68 961042
    D. Philipps 10/16/68 916042

8.____

9. Campbell 11/21/72 624856

    A. Campbell 11/21/72 624856
    B. Campbell 11/21/72 624586
    C. Campbell 11/21/72 624686
    D. Campbel 11/21/72 624856

9.____

10. Patterson 9/18/71 76199176

    A. Patterson 9/18/72 76191976
    B. Patterson 9/18/71 76199176
    C. Patterson 9/18/72 76199176
    D. Patterson 9/18/71 76919176

10.____

Questions 11-15.

DIRECTIONS: Questions 11 through 15 consist of groups of numbers and letters which you are to compare. For each question, you are to choose the option (A, B, C, or D) in Column II which *EXACTLY* matches the group of numbers and letters given in Column I.

SAMPLE QUESTION

Column I	Column II
B92466	A. B92644
	B. B94266
	C. A92466
	D. B92466

The correct answer is D. Only option D in Column II shows the group of numbers and letters *EXACTLY* as it appears in Column I. Now answer Questions 11 through 15 in the same manner.

	Column I	Column II
11.	925AC5	A. 952CA5
		B. 925AC5
		C. 952AC5
		D. 925CA6

12.   Y006925

A. Y060925
B. Y006295
C. Y006529
D. Y006925

13.   J236956

A. J236956
B. J326965
C. J239656
D. J932656

14.   AB6952

A. AB6952
B. AB9625
C. AB9652
D. AB6925

15.   X259361

A. X529361
B. X259631
C. X523961
D. X259361

Questions 16-25.

DIRECTIONS: Each of Questions 16 through 25 consists of three lines of code letters and three lines of numbers. The numbers on each line should correspond with the code letters on the same line in accordance with the table below.

Code Letter	S	V	W	A	Q	M	X	E	G	K
Corresponding Number	0	1	2	3	4	5	6	7	8	9

On some of the lines, an error exists in the coding. Compare the letters and numbers in each question carefully. If you find an error or errors on:
    only *one* of the lines in the question, mark your answer A;
    any *two* lines in the question, mark your answer B;
    all *three* lines in the question, mark your answer C;
    none of the lines in the question, mark your answer D.

SAMPLE QUESTION

WQGKSXG   2489068
XEKVQMA   6591453
KMAESXV   9527061

In the above example, the first line is correct since each code letter listed has the correct corresponding number. On the second line, an error exists because code letter E should have the number 7 instead of the number 5. On the third line an error exists because the code letter A should have the number 3 instead of the number 2. Since there are errors in two of the three lines, the correct answer is B. Now answer Questions 16 through 25 in the same manner.

16.   SWQEKGA   0247983   16._____
      KEAVSXM   9731065
      SSAXGKQ   0036894

17.   QAMKMVS   4259510   17._____
      MGGEASX   5897306
      KSWMKWS   9125920

18.	WKXQWVE	2964217	18.___
	QKXXQVA	4966413	
	AWMXGVS	3253810	
19.	GMMKASE	8559307	19.___
	AWVSKSW	3210902	
	QAVSVGK	4310189	
20.	XGKQSMK	6894049	20.___
	QSVKEAS	4019730	
	GSMXKMV	8057951	
21.	AEKMWSG	3195208	21.___
	MKQSVQK	5940149	
	XGQAEVW	6843712	
22.	XGMKAVS	6858310	22.___
	SKMAWEQ	0953174	
	GVMEQSA	8167403	
23.	VQSKAVE	1489317	23.___
	WQGKAEM	2489375	
	MEGKAWQ	5689324	
24.	XMQVSKG	6541098	24.___
	QMEKEWS	4579720	
	KMEVKGA	9571983	
25.	GKVAMEW	8912572	25.___
	AXMVKAE	3651937	
	KWAGMAV	9238531	

Questions 26-35.

DIRECTIONS: Each of Questions 26 through 35 consists of a column of figures. For each question, add the column of figures and choose the correct answer from the four choices given.

26. 5,665.43
    2,356.69
    6,447.24
    <u>7,239.65</u>

    A. 20,698.01   B. 21,709.01
    C. 21,718.01   D. 22,609.01

26.___

27. 817,209.55
    264,354.29
     82,368.76
    <u>849,964.89</u>

    A. 1,893,997.49   B. 1,989,988.39
    C. 2,009,077.39   D. 2,013,897,49

27.___

28.　156,366.89
　　　249,973.23
　　　823,229.49
　　　 56,869.45

　　A.　1,286,439.06　　　　　B.　1,287,521.06
　　C.　1,297,539.06　　　　　D.　1,296,421.06

28.____

29.　 23,422.15
　　　149,696.24
　　　238,377.53
　　　 86,289.79
　　　505,544.63

　　A.　989,229.34　　　　　　B.　999,879.34
　　C.　1,003,330.34　　　　　D.　1,023,329.34

29.____

30.　2,468,926.70
　　　 656,842.28
　　　　49,723.15
　　　 832,369.59

　　A.　3,218,061.72　　　　　B.　3,808,092.72
　　C.　4,007,861.72　　　　　D.　4,818,192.72

30.____

31.　　524,201.52
　　　7,775,678.51
　　　8,345,299.63
　　　40,628,898.08
　　　31,374,670.07

　　A.　88,646,647.81　　　　B.　88,646,747.91
　　C.　88,648,647.91　　　　D.　88,648,747.81

31.____

32.　6,824,829.40
　　　 682,482.94
　　　5,542,015.27
　　　 775,678.51
　　　7,732,507.25

　　A.　21,557,513.37　　　　B.　21,567,513.37
　　C.　22,567,503.37　　　　D.　22,567,513.37

32.____

33.　22,109,405.58
　　　6,097,093.43
　　　5,050,073.99
　　　8,118,050.05
　　　4,313,980.82

　　A.　45,688,593.87　　　　B.　45,688,603.87
　　C.　45,689,593.87　　　　D.　45,689,603.87

33.____

34.　79,324,114.19
　　　99,848,129.74
　　　43,331,653.31
　　　41,610,207.14

34.____

A. 264,114,104.38   B. 264,114,114.38
C. 265,114,114.38   D. 265,214,104.38

35.   33,729,653.94
        5,959,342.58
       26,052,715.47
        4,452,669.52
        7,079,953.59

A. 76,374,334.10   B. 76,375,334.10
C. 77,274,335.10   D. 77,275,335.10

Questions 36-40.

DIRECTIONS: Each of Questions 36 through 40 consists of a single number in Column I and four options in Column II. For each question, you are to choose the option (A, B, C, or D) in Column II which *EXACTLY* matches the number in Column I.

SAMPLE QUESTION

Column I   Column II
5965121   A.   5956121
              B.   5965121
              C.   5966121
              D.   5965211

The correct answer is B. Only option B shows the number *EXACTLY* as it appears in Column I. Now answer Questions 36 through 40 in the same manner.

Column I   Column II
36.   9643242   A.   9643242
                    B.   9462342
                    C.   9642442
                    D.   9463242

37.   3572477   A.   3752477
                    B.   3725477
                    C.   3572477
                    D.   3574277

38.   5276101   A.   5267101
                    B.   5726011
                    C.   5271601
                    D.   5276101

39.   4469329   A.   4496329
                    B.   4469329
                    C.   4496239
                    D.   4469239

40.   2326308   A.   2236308
                    B.   2233608
                    C.   2326308
                    D.   2323608

KEY (CORRECT ANSWERS)

1.	D	11.	B	21.	A	31.	D
2.	A	12.	D	22.	C	32.	A
3.	B	13.	A	23.	B	33.	B
4.	D	14.	A	24.	D	34.	A
5.	B	15.	D	25.	A	35.	C
6.	C	16.	D	26.	B	36.	A
7.	A	17.	C	27.	D	37.	C
8.	C	18.	A	28.	A	38.	D
9.	A	19.	D	29.	C	39.	B
10.	B	20.	B	30.	C	40.	C

TEST 2

Questions 1-5.

DIRECTIONS: Each of Questions 1 through 5 consists of a name and a dollar amount. In each question, the name and dollar amount in Column II should be an exact copy of the name and dollar amount in Column I. If there is:

a mistake only in the name, mark your answer A;
a mistake only in the dollar amount, mark your answer B;
a mistake in both the name and the dollar amount, mark your answer C;
no mistake in either the name or the dollar amount, mark your answer D.

SAMPLE QUESTION

Column I	Column II
George Peterson	George Petersson
$125.50	$125.50

Compare the name and dollar amount in Column II with the name and dollar amount in Column I. The name *Petersson* in Column II is spelled *Peterson* in Column I. The amount is the same in both columns. Since there is a mistake only in the name, the answer to the sample question is A.

Now answer Questions 1 through 5 in the same manner.

Column I	Column II	
1. Susanne Shultz $3440	Susanne Schultz $3440	1.___
2. Anibal P. Contrucci $2121.61	Anibel P. Contrucci $2112.61	2.___
3. Eugenio Mendoza $12.45	Eugenio Mendozza $12.45	3.___
4. Maurice Gluckstadt $4297	Maurice Gluckstadt $4297	4.___
5. John Pampellonne $4656.94	John Pammpellonne $4566.94	5.___

Questions 6-11.

DIRECTIONS: Each of Questions 6 through 11 consists of a set of names and addresses which you are to compare. In each question, the name and addresses in Column II should be an *EXACT* copy of the name and address in Column I. If there is:

a mistake only in the name, mark your answer A;
a mistake only in the address, mark your answer B;
a mistake in both the name and address, mark your answer C;
no mistake in either the name or address, mark your answer D.

SAMPLE QUESTION

Column I	Column II
Michael Filbert	Michael Filbert
456 Reade Street	645 Reade Street
New York, N.	New York, N . Y. 10013

Since there is a mistake only in the address (the street number should be 456 instead of 645), the answer to the sample question is B.

Now answer Questions 6 through 11 in the same manner.

	Column I	Column II	

6. Hilda Goettelmann   Hilda Goettelman   6.____
    55 Lenox Rd.   55 Lenox Ave.
    Brooklyn, N. Y. 11226   Brooklyn, N. Y. 11226

7. Arthur Sherman   Arthur Sharman   7.____
    2522 Batchelder St.   2522 Batcheder St.
    Brooklyn, N. Y. 11235   Brooklyn, N. Y. 11253

8. Ralph Barnett   Ralph Barnett   8.____
    300 West 28 Street   300 West 28 Street
    New York, New York 10001 New York, New York 10001

9. George Goodwin   George Godwin   9.____
    135 Palmer Avenue   135 Palmer Avenue
    Staten Island, New York 10302   Staten Island, New York 10302

10. Alonso Ramirez   Alonso Ramirez   10.____
    232 West 79 Street   223 West 79 Street
    New York, N. Y. 10024   New York, N. Y. 10024

11. Cynthia Graham   Cynthia Graham   11.____
    149-35 83 Street   149-35 83 Street
    Howard Beach, N. Y. 11414 Howard Beach, N. Y. 11414

Questions 12-20.

DIRECTIONS: Questions 12 through 20 are problems in subtraction. For each question do
              the subtraction and select your answer from the four choices given.

12.   232,921.85   12.____
      -179,587.68

        A.   52,433.17   B.   52,434.17
        C.   53,334.17   D.   53,343.17

13.   5,531,876.29   13.____
      -3,897,158.36

        A.   1,634,717.93   B.   1,644,718.93
        C.   1,734,717.93   D.   1,734,718.93

14.   1,482,658.22   14.____
      - 937,925.76

        A.   544,633.46   B.   544,732.46
        C.   545,632.46   D.   545,732.46

15.   937,828.17   15.____
      -259,673.88

        A.   678,154.29   B.   679,154.29
        C.   688,155.39   D.   699,155.39

16. 760,412.38
    -263,465.95

    A. 496,046.43   B. 496,946.43
    C. 496,956.43   D. 497,046.43

16.__

17. 3,203,902.26
    -2,933,087.96

    A. 260,814.30   B. 269,824.30
    C. 270,814.30   D. 270,824.30

17.__

18. 1,023,468.71
    - 934,678.88

    A. 88,780.83   B. 88,789.83
    C. 88,880.83   D. 88,889.83

18.__

19. 831,549.47
    -772,814.78

    A. 58,734.69   B. 58,834.69
    C. 59,735,69   D. 59,834.69

19.__

20. 6,306,281.74
    -3,617,376.75

    A. 2,687,904.99   B. 2,688,904.99
    C. 2,689,804.99   D. 2,799,905.99

20.__

Questions 21-30.

DIRECTIONS: Each of Questions 21 through 30 consists of three lines of code letters and three lines of numbers. The numbers on each line should correspond with the code letters on the same line in accordance with the table below.

Code Letter	J	U	B	T	Y	D	K	R	L	P
Corresponding Number	0	1	2	3	4	5	6	7	8	9

On some of the lines, an error exists in the coding. Compare the letters and numbers in each question carefully. If you find an error or errors on:
    only *one* of the lines in the question, mark your answer A;
    any *two* lines in the question, mark your answer B;
    all *three* lines in the question, mark your answer C;
    none of the lines in the question, mark your answer D.

SAMPLE QUESTION

BJRPYUR   2079417
DTBPYKJ   5328460
YKLDBLT   4685283

In the above sample the first line is correct since each code letter listed has the correct corresponding number. On the second line, an error exists because code letter P should have the number 9 instead of the number 8. The third line is correct since each code letter listed has the correct corresponding number. Since there is an error in *one* of the three lines, the correct answer is A.

Now answer Questions 21 through 30 in the same manner.

21.	BYPDTJL	2495308	21.____
	PLRDTJU	9815301	
	DTJRYLK	5207486	

22.	RPBYRJK	7934706	22.____
	PKTYLBU	9624821	
	KDLPJYR	6489047	

23.	TPYBUJR	3942107	23.____
	BYRKPTU	2476931	
	DUKPYDL	5169458	

24.	KBYDLPL	6345898	24.____
	BLRKBRU	2876261	
	JTULDYB	0318542	

25.	LDPYDKR	8594567	25.____
	BDKDRJL	2565708	
	BDRPLUJ	2679810	

26.	PLRLBPU	9858291	26.____
	LPYKRDJ	8936750	
	TDKPDTR	3569527	

27.	RKURPBY	7617924	27.____
	RYUKPTJ	7426930	
	RTKPTJD	7369305	

28.	DYKPBJT	5469203	28.____
	KLPJBTL	6890238	
	TKPLBJP	3698209	

29.	BTPRJYL	2397148	29.____
	LDKUTYR	8561347	
	YDBLRPJ	4528190	

30.	ULPBKYT	1892643	30.____
	KPDTRBJ	6953720	
	YLKJPTB	4860932	

KEY (CORRECT ANSWERS)

1.	A		16.	B
2.	C		17.	C
3.	A		18.	B
4.	D		19.	A
5.	C		20.	B
6.	C		21.	B
7.	C		22.	C
8.	D		23.	D
9.	A		24.	B
10.	B		25.	A
11.	D		26.	C
12.	C		27.	A
13.	A		28.	D
14.	B		29.	B
15.	A		30.	D

SPELLING

SAMPLE QUESTION

DIRECTIONS: The spelling test is designed to resemble a proofreading task. You are presented with a passage. Each line of the passage is considered one test question. You are to read the passage and indicate how many spelling errors are contained in each line. In some cases, a spelling error will consist of the use of the wrong form of a word that has several correct spellings. The different correct spellings of such words have different meanings, for example "to," "two," and "too." Be sure that you look for these kinds of errors. *PRINT THE LETTER OF THE CORRECT ANSWER IN THE SPACE AT THE RIGHT.*

KEY

A = The line contains no spelling errors.
B = There is one (1) spelling error in the line.
C = There are two (2) spelling errors in the line.
D = There are three (3) or more spelling errors in the line.

1. The main reasons for in-service training are to inprove the work being done by

2. employees in there present jobs and to meet the system and program goals of the

3. agency. It is the responsability of managers to suport and encourage teh use of

4. skills learned in training classes. In-service training will be done during normal work

5. hours and will be paied for by the employer.

KEY (CORRECT ANSWERS)

1. The correct answer is B. There is one spelling error. The word "improve" is misspelled as "inprove".

2. The correct answer is B. The word "there" is not spelled correctly for the use of the word in this sentence. In this case, we need the plural, possessive pronoun "their", so one spelling error is found in this line.

3. The correct answer is D. There are three misspelled words in this line: "responsibility," "support," and "the".

4. The correct answer is A. This line contains no spelling errors.

5. The correct answer is B. This line contains one spelling error. The word "paied" is misspelled and should be "paid" or "payed". Both are acceptable forms though "paid" is probably more commonly used.

SPELLING
EXAMINATION SECTION
TEST 1

DIRECTIONS: One word in each lettered group is misspelled. Indicate the letter of the misspelled word in the space at the right. Mark "E" if all are spelled correctly.

1. A. sacriligious   B. ingenius   C. advantageous   D. ingenuous   1.____

2. A. apparrel   B. barrel   C. quarrel   D. sorrel   2.____

3. A. carousal   B. cannester   C. carrousel   D. cygnet   3.____

4. A. preliminary   B. cemetary   C. seminary   D. eleemosynary   4.____

5. A. croquet   B. kimono   C. cocoanut   D. carom   5.____

6. A. chattel   B. privelege   C. convenience   D. immerse   6.____

7. A. resiliant   B. aspirant   C. adherent   D. conversant   7.____

8. A. sacrilege   B. entourage   C. demurage   D. persiflage   8.____

9. A. disappoint   B. dissatisfy   C. dessicate   D. dissuade   9.____

10. A. fallacy   B. fantasy   C. ecstacy   D. hypocrisy   10.____

11. A. elegible   B. illegible   C. intelligible   D. irascible   11.____

12. A. emission   B. omission   C. incision   D. comission   12.____

13. A. narrate   B. exaggerrate   C. disintegrate   D. hyphenate   13.____

14. A. chagrined   B. humbugged   C. kidnapped   D. fidgetted   14.____

15. A. flaccid   B. succinct   C. rancid   D. accrid   15.____

16. A. forehead   B. foresworn   C. foresight   D. forerunner   16.____

17. A. guard   B. language   C. guarantee   D. guage   17.____

18. A. embarrassed   B. harrassed   C. terraced   D. harnessed   18.____

19. A. persuade   B. imperterbable   C. pursuit   D. purport   19.____

20. A. innuendo   B. inoculate   C. inovation   D. innocuous   20.____

21. A. weird   B. inviegle   C. siege   D. seized   21.____

22. A. ratify   B. rarefy   C. liquify   D. ramify   22.____

23. A. muscles   B. mussels   C. missals   D. missies   23.____

24. A. Philippines   B. penicillen   C. patrolling   D. prairie   24.____

25. A. questionaire   B. fanfare   C. flair   D. solitaire   25.____

KEY (CORRECT ANSWERS)

1. A   sacrilegious
2. A   apparel
3. B   cannister
4. B   cemetery
5. E

6. B   privilege
7. A   resilient
8. C   demurrage
9. C   desiccate
10. C   ecstasy

11. A   eligible
12. D   commission
13. B   exaggerate
14. D   fidgeted
15. D   acrid

16. B   forsworn
17. D   gauge
18. B   harassed
19. B   imperturbable
20. C   innovation

21. B   inveigle
22. C   liquefy
23. D   missiles
24. B   penicillin
25. A   questionnaire

TEST 2

DIRECTIONS: Two words in each lettered group are INCORRECTLY spelled. Indicate the two
misspelled words in each group in the space at the right.

	A.		B.		C.		D.		
1.	A. accidently	B. apology	C. description	D. devide	1.____
2.	A. accomodate	B. apparatus	C. business	D. desireable	2.____
3.	A. arguement	B. conscience	C. dining	D. convience	3.____
4.	A. across	B. atheletics	C. changeable	D. dissapoint	4.____
5.	A. choose	B. disasterous	C. dissatisfied	D. courtecy	5.____
6.	A. all right	B. allready	C. almost	D. alltogether	6.____
7.	A. eighth	B. formerly	C. formaly	D. begining	7.____
8.	A. ninth	B. forty	C. embarrasment	D. ninty	8.____
9.	A. fourth	B. lose	C. noticable	D. enviroment	9.____
10.	A. grammer	B. irrelevent	C. weight	D. either	10.____
11.	A. familar	B. similiar	C. its	D. width	11.____
12.	A. occassionally	B. occurence	C. government	D. exceed	12.____
13.	A. labatory	B. necessary	C. outragous	D. paid	13.____
14.	A. dipthong	B. pamphlett	C. hoping	D. illegible	14.____
15.	A. beleive	B. concieve	C. quite	D. quiet	15.____
16.	A. benefited	B. preferable	C. wheather	D. grievious	16.____
17.	A. counterfeit	B. serviceable	C. conferance	D. confidentally	17.____
18.	A. quantity	B. quality	C. probally	D. libary	18.____
19.	A. recieve	B. decieve	C. perform	D. preferred	19.____
20.	A. reconize	B. seperate	C. truly	D. inter	20.____
21.	A. perfessor	B. useing	C. proceed	D. impede	21.____
22.	A. you're	B. it's	C. preceed	D. impeed	22.____
23.	A. possession	B. pursue	C. pursuade	D. religeous	23.____
24.	A. rhythm	B. schedule	C. repitition	D. usualy	24.____
25.	A. mileage	B. peaceable	C. minature	D. superintendant	25.____

KEY (CORRECT ANSWERS)

1. A,D   accidentally, divide
2. A,D   accommodate, desirable
3. A,D   argument, convenience
4. A,D   athletics, disappoint
5. B,D   disastrous, courtesy

6. B,D   already, altogether
7. C,D   formally, beginning
8. C,D   embarrassment, ninety
9. C,D   noticeable, environment
10. A,B   grammar, irrelevant

11. A,B   familiar, similar
12. A,B   occasionally, occurrence
13. A,C   laboratory, outrageous
14. A,B   diphthong, pamphlet
15. A,B   believe, conceive

16. C,D   whether, grievous
17. C,D   conference, confidentially
18. C,D   probably, library
19. A,B   receive, deceive
20. A,B   recognize, separate

21. A,B   professor, using
22. C,D   precede, impede
23. C,D   persuade, religious
24. C,D   repetition, usually
25. C,D   miniature, superintendent

———

TEST 3

DIRECTIONS: Two words in each lettered group are INCORRECTLY spelled. Indicate the two misspelled words in each group in the space at the right.

1.	A.	consolible	B.	libel	C.	inteligible	D.	irascible	1.____
2.	A.	beneficient	B.	correlative	C.	awful	D.	offeng	2.____
3.	A.	tractible	B.	malleable	C.	tracable	D.	exchangeable	3.____
4.	A.	inviegle	B.	weird	C.	seige	D.	seized	4.____
5.	A.	recommend	B.	saccharine	C.	dillemma	D.	millenium	5.____
6.	A.	dissipated	B.	loneliness	C.	incidently	D.	corroberate	6.____
7.	A.	advantageous	B.	ingenious	C.	facetous	D.	ingenous	7.____
8.	A.	inoculate	B.	innuendo	C.	inovation	D.	inocuous	8.____
9.	A.	embarassed	B.	harrassed	C.	harnessed	D.	terraced	9.____
10.	A.	monsignier	B.	mayorality	C.	saxophone	D.	liquefied	10.____
11.	A.	caravansery	B.	compulsary	C.	anniversary	D.	adversary	11.____
12.	A.	duteable	B.	scurilous	C.	beseech	D.	catechized	12.____
13.	A.	exaggerate	B.	narrate	C.	disintigrate	D.	hyphenate	13.____
14.	A.	ommission	B.	emission	C.	omnitient	D.	commission	14.____
15.	A.	persuit	B.	purser	C.	imperterbable	D.	purport	15.____
16.	A.	adherrent	B.	conversant	C.	resiliant	D.	aspirant	16.____
17.	A.	mussels	B.	missils	C.	missles	D.	muscles	17.____
18.	A.	palaver	B.	deffer	C.	profer	D.	prefer	18.____
19.	A.	million	B.	batallion	C.	pavillion	D.	stallion	19.____
20.	A.	inability	B.	intelligibility	C.	elligibility	D.	fallability	20.____
21.	A.	alottment	B.	equipment	C.	detrement	D.	installment	21.____
22.	A.	foresworn	B.	forehead	C.	forsight	D.	forerunner	22.____
23.	A.	guage	B.	language	C.	gaurantee	D.	guard	23.____
24.	A.	sorel	B.	apparrel	C.	barrel	D.	quarrel	24.____
25.	A.	questionaire	B.	flaire	C.	fanfare	D.	solitary	25.____

KEY (CORRECT ANSWERS)

1.	A,C	consolable, intelligible
2.	A,D	beneficent, offing
3.	A,C	tractable, traceable
4.	A,C	inveigle, siege
5.	C,D	dilemma, millennium
6.	C,D	incidentally, corroborate
7.	C,D	facetious, ingenious
8.	C,D	innovation, innocuous
9.	A,B	embarrassed, harassed
10.	A,B	monsignior, mayoralty
11.	A,B	caravansary, compulsory
12.	A,B	dutiable, scurrilous
13.	A,C	exaggerate, disintegrate
14.	A,C	omission, omniscient
15.	A,C	pursuit, imperturbable
16.	A,C	adherent, resilient
17.	B,C	missals, missiles
18.	B,C	defer, proffer
19.	B,C	battalion, pavilion
20.	C,D	eligibility, fallibility
21.	A,C	allotment, detriment
22.	A,C	forsworn, foresight
23.	A,C	gauge, guarantee
24.	A,B	sorrel, apparel
25.	A,B	questionnaire, flair

ARITHMETICAL REASONING
EXAMINATION SECTION
TEST 1

DIRECTIONS: Each question or incomplete statement is followed by several suggested answers or completions. Select the one that BEST answers the question or completes the statement. *PRINT THE LETTER OF THE CORRECT ANSWER IN THE SPACE AT THE RIGHT.*

1. If a secretary answered 28 phone calls and typed the addresses for 112 credit statements in one morning, what is the RATIO of phone calls answered to credit statements typed for that period of time?

    A. 1:4   B. 1:7   C. 2:3   D. 3:5

1.____

2. According to a suggested filing system, no more than 10 folders should be filed behind any one file guide and from 15 to 25 file guides should be used in each file drawer for easy finding and filing.
The MAXIMUM number of folders that a five-drawer file cabinet can hold to allow easy finding and filing is

    A. 550   B. 750   C. 1,100   D. 1,250

2.____

3. An employee had a starting salary of $19,353. He received a salary increase at the end of each year, and at the end of the seventh year his salary was $25,107.
What was his AVERAGE annual increase in salary over these seven years?

    A. $765   B. $807   C. $822   D. $858

3.____

4. The 55 typists and 28 senior clerks in a certain agency were paid a total of $1,457,400 in salaries in 2005.
If the average annual salary of a typist was $16,800, the average annual salary of a senior clerk was

    A. $19,050   B. $19,950   C. $20,100   D. $20,250

4.____

5. A typist has been given a three-page report to type. She has finished typing the first two pages. The first page has 283 words, and the second page has 366 words.
If the total report consists of 954 words, how many words will she have to type on the third page of the report?

    A. 202   B. 287   C. 305   D. 313

5.____

6. In one day, Clerk A processed 30% more forms than Clerk B, and Clerk C processed 1 1/4 as many forms as Clerk A.
If Clerk B processed 40 forms, how many more forms were processed by Clerk C than Clerk B?

    A. 12   B. 13   C. 21   D. 25

6.____

7. A clerk who earns a gross salary of $678 every 2 weeks has the following deductions taken from her paycheck: 15% for city, state, and federal taxes; 2 1/2% for Social Security; $1.95 for health insurance; and $9.00 for union dues.
The amount of her take-home pay is
    A. $429.60   B. $468.60   C. $497.40   D. $548.40

7.____

8. In 2002, an agency spent $400 to buy pencils at a cost of $1.00 a dozen.
If the agency used 3/4 of these pencils in 2002 and used the same number of pencils in 2003, how many more pencils did it have to buy to have enough pencils for all of 2003?
    A. 1,200   B. 2,400   C. 3,600   D. 4,800

8.____

9. A clerk who worked in Agency X earned the following salaries: $15,105 the first year, $15,750 the second year, and $16,440 the third year. Another clerk who worked in Agency Y for three years earned $15,825 a year for two years and $16,086 the third year.
The DIFFERENCE between the average salaries received by both clerks over a three-year period is
    A. $147   B. $153   C. $261   D. $423

9.____

10. An employee who works more than 40 hours in any week receives overtime payment for the extra hours at time and one-half (1 1/2 times) his hourly rate of pay. An employee who earns $13.60 an hour works a total of 45 hours during a certain week.
His TOTAL pay for that week would be
    A. $564.40   B. $612.00   C. $646.00   D. $824.00

10.____

11. Suppose that the amount of money spent for supplies in 2006 for a division in a city department was $156,500. This represented an increase of 12% over the amount spent for supplies for this division in 2005.
The amount of money spent for supplies for this division in 2005 was MOST NEARLY
    A. $139,730   B. $137,720   C. $143,460   D. $138,720

11.____

12. Suppose that a group of five clerks have been assigned to insert 24,000 letters into envelopes. The clerks perform this work at the following rates of speed: Clerk A, 1,100 letters an hour; Clerk B, 1,450 letters an hour; Clerk C, 1,200 letters an hour; Clerk D, 1,300 letters an hour; Clerk E, 1,250 letters an hour. At the end of two hours of work, Clerks C and D are assigned to another task.
From the time that Clerks C and D were taken off the assignment, the number of hours required for the remaining clerks to complete this assignment is

    A. less than 3 hours
    B. 3 hours
    C. more than 3 hours, but less than 4 hours
    D. more than 4 hours

12.____

13. The number 60 is 40% of
    A. 24   B. 84   C. 96   D. 150

13.____

14. If 3/8 of a number is 96, the number is
    A. 132   B. 36   C. 256   D. 156

14.____

15. A city department uses an average of 25 20-cent, 35 30-cent, and 350 40-cent postage stamps each day.
The TOTAL cost of stamps used by the department in a five-day period is

    A. $29.50   B. $155.50   C. $290.50   D. $777.50

    15.____

16. A city department issued 12,000 applications in 2000. The number of applications that the department issued in 1998 was 25% greater than the number it issued in 2000.
If the department issued 10% fewer applications in 1996 than it did in 1998, the number it issued in 1996 was

    A. 16,500   B. 13,500   C. 9,900   D. 8,100

    16.____

17. A clerk can add 40 columns of figures an hour by using an adding machine and 20 columns of figures an hour without using an adding machine.
The TOTAL number of hours it would take him to add 200 columns if he does 3/5 of the work by machine and the rest without the machine is

    A. 6   B. 7   C. 8   D. 9

    17.____

18. In 1997, a city department bought 500 dozen pencils at $1.20 per dozen. In 2000, only 75 percent as many pencils were bought as were bought in 1997, but the price was 20 percent higher than the 1997 price. The TOTAL cost of the pencils bought in 2000 was

    A. $540   B. $562.50   C. $720   D. $750

    18.____

19. A clerk is assigned to check the accuracy of the entries on 490 forms. He checks 40 forms an hour. After working one hour on this task, he is joined by another clerk, who checks these forms at the rate of 35 an hour.
The TOTAL number of hours required to do the entire assignment is

    A. 5   B. 6   C. 7   D. 8

    19.____

20. Assume that there are a total of 420 employees in a city agency. Thirty percent of the employees are clerks, and 1/7 are typists.
The DIFFERENCE between the number of clerks and the number of typists is

    A. 126   B. 66   C. 186   D. 80

    20.____

21. Assume that a duplicating machine produces copies of a bulletin at a cost of 2 cents per copy. The machine produces 120 copies of the bulletin per minute.
If the cost of producing a certain number of copies was $12, how many minutes of operation did it take the machine to produce this number of copies?

    A. 5   B. 2   C. 10   D. 6

    21.____

22. An assignment is completed by 32 clerks in 22 days. Assuming that all the clerks work at the same rate of speed, the number of clerks that would be needed to complete this assignment in 16 days is

    A. 27   B. 38   C. 44   D. 52

    22.____

23. A department head hired a total of 60 temporary employees to handle a seasonal increase in the department's workload. The following lists the number of temporary employees hired, their rates of pay, and the duration of their employment:
    One-third of the total were hired as clerks, each at the rate of $27,500 a year, for two months.
    30 percent of the total were hired as office machine operators, each at the rate of $31,500 a year, for four months.
    22 stenographers were hired, each at the rate of $30,000 a year, for three months.
    The total amount paid to these temporary employees was MOST NEARLY

    A. $1,780,000   B. $450,000
    C. $650,000   D. $390,000

23.____

24. Assume that there are 2,300 employees in a city agency. Also, assume that five percent of these employees are accountants, that 80 percent of the accountants have college degrees, and that one-half of the accountants who have college degrees have five years of experience. Then, the number of employees in the agency who are accountants with college degrees and five years of experience is

    A. 46   B. 51   C. 460   D. 920

24.____

25. Assume that the regular 8-hour working day of a laborer is from 8 A.M. to 5 P.M., with an hour off for lunch. He earns a regular hourly rate of pay for these 8 hours and is paid at the rate of time-and-a-half for each hour worked after his regular working day.
    If, on a certain day, he works from 8 A.M. to 6 P.M., with an hour off for lunch, and earns $171, his regular hourly rate of pay is

    A. $16.30   B. $17.10   C. $18.00   D. $19.00

25.____

KEY (CORRECT ANSWERS)

1.	A		11.	A
2.	D		12.	B
3.	C		13.	D
4.	A		14.	C
5.	C		15.	D
6.	D		16.	B
7.	D		17.	B
8.	B		18.	A
9.	A		19.	C
10.	C		20.	B

21.	A
22.	C
23.	B
24.	A
25.	C

SOLUTIONS TO PROBLEMS

1. 28/112 is equivalent to 1:4

2. Maximum number of folders = (10)(25)(5) = 1250

3. Average annual increase = ($25,107-19,353) ÷ 7 = $822

4. $1,457,400 - (55)($16,800) = $533,400 = total amount paid to senior clerks. Average senior clerk's salary = $533,400 ÷ 28 = $19,050

5. Number of words on 3rd page = 954 - 283 - 366 = 305

6. Clerk A processed (40)(1.30) = 52 forms and clerk C processed (52)(1.25) = 65 forms. Finally, 65 - 40 = 25

7. Take-home pay = $678 - (.15)($678) - (.025)($678) - $1.95 - $9.00 = $548.40

8. (400)(12) = 4800 pencils. In 2002, (3/4)(4800) = 3600 were used, so that 1200 pencils were available at the beginning of 2003. Since 3600 pencils were also used in 2003, the agency had to buy 3600 - 1200 = 2400 pencils.

9. Average salary for clerk in Agency X = ($15,105+$15,750+$16,440)/3 = $15,765. Average salary for clerk in Agency Y = ($15,825+ $15,825+$16,086) ÷ 3 = $15,912. Difference in average salaries = $147.

10. Total pay = ($13.60)(40) + ($20.40)(5) = $646.00

11. In 2005, amount spent = $156,500 ÷ 1.12 ≈ $139,730 (Actual value = $139,732.1429)

12. At the end of 2 hours, (1100)(2) + (1450)(2) + (1200)(2) + (1300X2) + (1250X2) = 12,600 letters have been inserted into envelopes. The remaining 11,400 letters done by clerks A, B, and C will require 11,400 ÷ (1100+1450+1250) = 3 hours.

13. 60 ÷ .40 = 150

14. 96 ÷ 3/8 = (96)(8/3) = 256

15. Total cost = (5)[(25)(.20)+(35)(.30)+(350)(.40)]= $777.50

16. In 1998, (12,000) (1.25) = 15,000 applications were issued In 1996, (15,000)(.90) = 13,500 applications were issued

17. Total number of hours $=\dfrac{120}{40} + \dfrac{80}{20} = 7$

18. (.75)(500 dozen) = 375 dozen purchased in 2000 at a cost of ($1.20)(1.20) = $1.44 per dozen. Total cost for 2000 = ($1.44) (375) = $540

19. Total time = 1 hour + 450/75 hrs. = 7 hours

20. (.30)(420) - (1/7)(420) = 126 - 60 = 66

21. Cost per minute = (120)(.02) = $2.40. Then, $12 ÷ $2.40 = 5 minutes

22. (32)(22) ÷ 16 = 44 clerks

23. Total amount paid = (20)($27,500)(2/12) + (18)($31,500) (4/12) + (22)($30,000)(3/12) = $445,666.$\overline{6}$ ≈ $450,000

24. Number of accountants with college degrees and five years of experience = (2300)(.05)(.80)(1/2) = 46

25. Let x = regular hourly pay. Then, (8)(x) + (1)(1.5x) = $1.71 So, 9.5x = 171. Solving, x = $18

———

TEST 2

DIRECTIONS: Each question or incomplete statement is followed by several suggested answers or completions. Select the one that BEST answers the question or completes the statement. *PRINT THE LETTER OF THE CORRECT ANSWER IN THE SPACE AT THE RIGHT.*

1. Assume that you know the capacity of a filing cabinet, the extent of which it is filled, and the daily rate at which material is being added to the file.
   In order to estimate how many more days it will take for the cabinet to be filled to capacity, you should

   1.____

   A.   divide the extent to which the cabinet is filled by the daily rate
   B.   take the difference between the capacity of the cabinet and the material in it, and multiply the result by the daily rate of adding material
   C.   divide the daily rate of adding material by the difference between the capacity of the cabinet and the material in it
   D.   take the difference between the capacity of the cabinet and the material in it, and divide the result by the daily rate of adding material

2. Suppose you have been asked to compute the average salary earned in your department during the past year. For each of the divisions of the department, you are given the number of employees and the average salary.
   In order to find the requested overall average salary for the department, you should

   2.____

   A.   add the average salaries of the various divisions and divide the total by the number of divisions
   B.   multiply the number of employees in each division by the corresponding average salary, add the results and divide the total by the number of employees in the department
   C.   add the average salaries of the various divisions and divide the total by the total number of employees in the department
   D.   multiply the sum of the average salaries of the various divisions by the total number of divisions and divide the resulting product by the total number of employees in the department

3. Suppose that a group of six clerks has been assigned to assemble the duplicated pages of a report into completed copies. After four hours of work, they have been able to complete one-third of the job.
   In order to assemble all the remaining copies in three more hours of work, the number of clerks which will have to be added to the original six, assuming that all the clerks assigned to this task work at the same rate of speed, is

   3.____

   A.   10   B.   16   C.   2   D.   6

4. A study of the grades of students in a certain college revealed that in 2005, 15% fewer students received a passing grade in mathematics than in 2004, whereas in 2006 the number of students passing mathematics increased 15% over 2005.
   On the basis of this study, it would be MOST accurate to conclude that

   4.____

   A.   the same percentage of students passed mathematics in 2004 as in 2006
   B.   of the three years studied, the greatest percentage of students passed mathematics in 2006

C.   the percentage of students who passed mathematics in 2006 was less than the percentage passing this subject in 2004

D.   the percentage of students passing mathematics in 2004 was 15% greater than the percentage of students passing this subject in 2006

5.   A city department employs 1,400 people, of whom 35% are clerks and 1/8 are stenographers.

     The number of employees in the department who are neither clerks nor stenographers is

     A.   640   B.   665   C.   735   D.   760

6.   Assume that there are 190 papers to be filed and that Clerk A and Clerk B are assigned to file these papers. If Clerk A files 40 papers more than Clerk B, then the number of papers that Clerk A files is

     A.   75   B.   110   C.   115   D.   150

7.   A stock clerk had on hand the following items:
       500 pads, each worth 16 cents
       130 pencils, each worth 12 cents
       50 dozen rubber bands, worth 8 cents a dozen
     If, from this stock, he issued 125 pads, 45 pencils, and 48 rubber bands, the value of the remaining stock would be

     A. $25.72   B. $27.80   C. $70.52   D. $73.88

8.   In a particular agency, there were 160 accidents in 2002. Of these accidents, 75% were due to unsafe acts and the rest were due to unsafe conditions. In the following year, a special safety program was established. The number of accidents in 2004 due to unsafe acts was reduced to 35% of what it had been in 2002.
     How many accidents due to unsafe acts were there in 2004?

     A.   20   B.   36   C.   42   D.   56

9.   At the end of every month, the petty cash fund of Agency A is reimbursed for payments made from the fund during the month. During the month of February, the amounts paid from the fund were entered on receipts as follows: 10 bus fares of $1.40 each and one taxi fare of $14.00. At the end of the month, the money left in the fund was in the following denominations: 60 one-dollar bills, 16 quarters, 40 dimes, and 80 nickels.
     If the petty cash fund is reduced by 20% for the following month, how much money will there be available in the petty cash fund for March?

     A. $44   B. $80   C. $86   D. $100

10.   An employee worked on a job for 6 weeks, 5 days per week, and 8 hours per day.
     How many hours did he work on the job?

     A.   40   B.   48   C.   55   D.   240

11.   Divide 35 by .7.

     A.   5   B.   42   C.   50   D.   245

5.___

6.___

7.___

8.___

9.___

10.___

11.___

12. .1% of 25 =   12.____

    A. .025   B. .25   C. 2.5   D. 25

13. In a city agency, 80 percent of the total number of employees are more than 25 years of   13.____
    age and 65 percent of the total number of employees are high school graduates.
    The SMALLEST possible percent of employees who are both high school graduates
    and more than 25 years of age is

    A. 35%   B. 45%   C. 55%   D. 65%

14. Two clerical units, X and Y, each having a different number of clerks, are assigned to file   14.____
    registration cards. It takes Unit X, which contains 8 clerks, 21 days to file the same num-
    ber of cards that Unit Y can file in 28 days. It is also a fact that Unit X can file 174,528
    cards in 72 days.
    Assuming that all the clerks in both units work at the same rate of speed, the number
    of cards which can be filed by Unit Y in 144 days, if 4 more clerks are added to the staff
    of Unit Y, is MOST NEARLY

    A. 392,000   B. 436,000   C. 523,000   D. 669,000

15. Assume that two machines, each costing $14,750, were purchased for your office. Each   15.____
    machine requires the services of an operator at a salary of $2,000 per month. These
    machines are to replace six clerks, two of whom earn $1,550 per month each, and four of
    whom earn $1,700 per month each.
    The number of months it will take for the cost of the machines to be made up from the
    savings in salaries is

    A. less than four   B. four
    C. five   D. more than five

16. Suppose that the amount of stationery used by your department in August decreased by   16.____
    16% as compared with the amount used in July, and that the amount used in September
    increased by 25% as compared with the amount used in August.
    The amount of stationery used in September as compared with the amount used in
    July is

    A. greater by 5 percent   B. less by 5 percent
    C. greater by 9 percent   D. the same

17. An employee earns $48 a day and works 5 days a week.   17.____
    He will earn $2,160 in _____ weeks.

    A. 5   B. 7   C. 8   D. 9

18. In a certain bureau, the entire staff consists of 1 senior supervisor, 2 supervisors, 6   18.____
    assistant supervisors, and 54 associate workers.
    The percent of the staff who are not associate workers is MOST NEARLY

    A. 14   B. 21   C. 27   D. 32

19. In a certain bureau, five employees each earn $1,000 a month, another 3 employees   19.____
    each earn $2,200 a month, and another two employees each earn $1,400 a month.
    The monthly payroll for these employees is

    A. $3,600   B. $8,800   C. $11,400   D. $14,400

20. An employee contributes 5% of his salary to the pension fund. 20.____
If his salary is $1,200 a month, the amount of his contribution to the pension fund in a year is

    A. $480   B. $720   C. $960   D. $1,200

21. The number of square feet in an area that is 50 feet long and 30 feet wide is 21.____

    A. 80   B. 150   C. 800   D. 1,500

22. A farm hand was paid a weekly wage of $332.16 for a 48-hour work week. As a result of 22.____
a new labor contract, he is paid $344.96 a week for a 44-hour work week with time and one-half pay for time worked in excess of 44 hours in any work week.
If he continues to work 48 hours weekly under the new contract, the amount by which his average hourly rate for a 48-hour work week under the new contract exceeds the hourly rate previously paid him lies between _____ and _____ cents, inclusive.

    A. 91;100   B. 101;110   C. 111;120   D. 121;130

23. Each side of a square room, which is being used as an office, measures 66 feet. The 23.____
floor of the room is divided by six traffic aisles, each aisle being six feet wide. Three of the aisles run parallel to the east and west sides of the room, and the other three run parallel to the north and south sides of the room, so that the remaining floor space is divided into 16 equal sections. If all of the floor space which is not being used for traffic aisles is occupied by desk and chair sets, and each set takes up 24 square feet of floor space, the number of desk and chair sets in the room is

    A. 80   B. 64   C. 36   D. 96

24. In 2005, a city agency bought 12,000 envelopes at $4.00 per hundred. In 2006, the price 24.____
of envelopes purchased was 40 percent higher than the 2005 price, but only 60 percent as many envelopes were bought.
The total cost of the envelopes purchased in 2006 was MOST NEARLY

    A. $250   B. $320   C. $400   D. $480

25. In a city agency, 25 percent of the women employees and 50 percent of the men employ- 25.____
ees attended a general staff meeting.
If 48 percent of all the employees in the agency are women, the percentage of all the employees who attended the meeting is

    A. 36%   B. 37%   C. 38%   D. 75%

_____

KEY (CORRECT ANSWERS)

1.	D		11.	C
2.	B		12.	A
3.	A		13.	B
4.	C		14.	A
5.	C		15.	C
6.	C		16.	A
7.	D		17.	D
8.	C		18.	A
9.	B		19.	D
10.	D		20.	B

21.	D
22.	D
23.	D
24.	C
25.	C

SOLUTIONS TO PROBLEMS

1. To determine number of days required to fill cabinet to capacity, subtract material in it from capacity amount, then divide by daily rate of adding material. Example: A cabinet already has 10 folders in it, and the capacity is 100 folders. Suppose 5 folders per day are added. Number of days to fill to capacity = (100-10) ÷ 5 = 18

2. To determine overall average salary, multiply number of employees in each division by that division's average salary, add results, then divide by total number of employees. Example: Division A has 4 employees with average salary of $40,000; division B has 6 employees with average salary of $36,000; division C has 2 employees with average salary of $46,000. Average salary = [(4)($40,000)+(6)($36,000)+(2)($46,000)] / 12 = $39,000

3. (6)(4) = 24 clerk-hours. Since only one-third of work has been done, (24) (3) - 24 = 48 clerk-hours remain. Then, 48 3 = 16 clerks. Thus, 16 - 6 = 10 additional clerks.

4. The percentage of students passing math in 2006 was less than the percentage of those passing math in 2004. Example: Suppose 400 students passed math in 2004. Then, (400)(.85) = 340 passed in 2005. Finally, (340)(1.15) = 391 passed in 2006.

5. 1400 - (.35)(1400) - (1/8)(1400) = 735

6. Let x = number of papers filed by clerk A, x-40 = number of papers filed by clerk B. Then, x + (x-40) = 190 Solving, x = 115

7. (500-125)(.16) + (130-45)(.12) + (50 - 48/12)(.08) = $60.00 + $10.20 + $3.68 = $73.88

8. (160)(.75) = 120 accidents due to unsafe acts in 2002. In 2004, (120)(.35) = 42 accidents due to unsafe acts

9. Original amount at beginning of February in the fund = (10)($1.40) + (1)($14.00) + (60)($1) + (16)(.25) + (40)(.10) + (80)(.05) = $100. Finally, for March, ($100)(.80) = $80 will be available

10. Total hours = (6)(5)(8) = 240

11. 35 ÷ .7 = 50

12. .1% of 25 = (.001)(25) = .025

13. Let A = percent of employees who are at least 25 years old and B = percent of employees who are high school graduates. Also, let N = percent of employees who fit neither category and J = percent of employees who are in both categories.
Then, 100 = A + B + N - J. Substituting, 100 = 80 + 65 + N - J To minimize J, let N = 0. So, 100 = 80 + 65 + 0 - J. Solving, J = 45

14. Let Y = number of clerks in Unit Y. Then, (8)(21) = (4)(28), so Y = 6. Unit X has 8 clerks who can file 174,528 cards in 72 flays; thus, each clerk in Unit X can file 174,528 ÷ 72 ÷ 8 = 303 cards per day. Adding 4 clerks to Unit Y will yield 10 clerks in that unit. Since their rate is equal to that of Unit X, the clerks in Unit Y will file, in 144 days, is (303)(10)(144) = 436,320 ≈ 436,000 cards.

15. Let x = required number of months. The cost of the machines in x months = (2)(14,750) + (2)(2000)(x) = 29,500 + 4000x. The savings in salaries for the displaced clerks = x[(2)(1550) +(4)(1700)] = 9900x. Thus, 29,500 + 4000x = 9900x. Solving, x = 5. So, five months will elapse in order to achieve a savings in cost.

16. Let x = amount used in July, so that .84x = amount used in August. For September, the amount used = (.84x)(1.25) = 1.05x. This means the amount used in September is 5% more than the amount used in July.

17. Each week he earns ($48)(5) = $240. Then, $2160 ÷ $240 = 9 weeks

18. (1+2+6) ÷ 63 = 1/7 ≈ 14%

19. Monthly payroll = (5)($1000) + (3)($2200) + (2)($1400) = $14,400

20. Yearly contribution to pension fund = (12)($1200)(.05) = $720

21. (50')(30') = 1500 sq.ft.

22. Old rate = 332.16 ÷ 48 = 6.92 (48 hours)
    New rate = 344.96 (44 hours)
    Overtime rate = 344.96 ÷ 44 = 7.75/hr. x 1.5 x 4 = 46.48
    344.96 + 46.48 = 391.44
    391.44 ÷ 48 = 8.15
    815 - 692 = 123 cents an hour more

23. Each of the 16 sections is a square with side [66'-(3)(6')] ÷ 4 = 12'. So each section contains (12')(12') = 144 sq.ft.
    The number of desk and chair sets = (144 ÷ 24) (16) = 96

24. In 2006, (.60)(12,000) = 7200 envelopes were bought and the price per hundred was ($4.00)(1.40) = $5.60. The total cost = (5.60)(72) = $403.20 ≈ $400

25. (.25)(.48) + (.50)(.52) = .38 = 38%

TEST 3

1. According to one suggested filing system, no more than 12 folders should be filed behind any one file guide and from 10 to 20 file guides should be used in each file drawer. Based on this filing system, the MAXIMUM number of folders that a four-drawer file cabinet can hold is   1.___

   A. 240   B. 480   C. 960   D. 1,200

2. A certain office uses three different forms. Last year, it used 3,500 copies of Form L, 6,700 copies of Form M, and 10,500 copies of Form P. This year, the office expects to decrease the use of each of these forms by 5%. The TOTAL number of these three forms which the office expects to use this year is   2.___

   A. 10,350   B. 16,560   C. 19,665   D. 21,735

3. The hourly rate of pay for a certain part-time employee is computed by dividing his yearly salary rate by the number of hours in the work year. The employee's yearly salary rate is $18,928, and there are 1,820 hours in the work year.
   If this employee works 18 hours during one week, his TOTAL earnings for these 18 hours are   3.___

   A. $180.00   B. $183.60   C. $187.20   D. $190.80

4. Assume that the regular work week of an employee is 35 hours and that the employee is paid for any extra hours worked according to the following schedule. For hours worked in excess of 35 hours, up to and including 40 hours, the employee receives his regular hourly rate of pay. For hours worked in excess of 40 hours, the employee receives 1 1/2 times his hourly rate of pay.
   If the employee's hourly rate of pay is $11.20 and he works 43 hours during a certain week, his TOTAL pay for the week would be   4.___

   A. $481.60   B. $498.40   C. $556.00   D. $722.40

5. A clerk divided his 35 hour work week as follows:
       1/5 of his time in sorting mail;
       1/2 of his time in filing letters; and
       1/7 of his time in reception work.
   The rest of his time was devoted to messenger work. The percentage of time spent on messenger work by the clerk during the week was MOST NEARLY   5.___

   A. 6%   B. 10%   C. 14%   D. 16%

6. A city department has set up a computing unit and has rented 5 computing machines at a yearly rental of $700 per machine. In addition, the cost to the department for the maintenance and repair of each of these machines is $50 per year. Five computing machine operators, each receiving an annual salary of $15,000, and a supervisor, who receives $19,000 a year, have been assigned to this unit. This unit will perform the work previously performed by 10 employees whose combined salary was $162,000 a year.
   On the basis of these facts, the savings that will result from the operation of this computing unit for 5 years will be MOST NEARLY   6.___

   A. $250,000   B. $320,000   C. $330,000   D. $475,000

7. Twelve clerks are assigned to enter certain data on index cards. This number of clerks   7._____
could perform the task in 18 days. After these clerks have worked on this assignment for
6 days, 4 more clerks are added to the staff to do this work.
Assuming that all the clerks work at the same rate of speed, the entire task, instead of
taking 18 days, will be performed in _____ days.

    A. 9   B. 12   C. 15   D. 16

8. Suppose that a file cabinet, which has a capacity of 3,000 cards, now contains approxi-   8._____
mately 2,200 cards. Cards are added to the file at the average rate of 30 cards a day.
To find the number of days it will take to fill the cabinet to capacity,

    A.   divide 3,000 by 30
    B.   divide 2,200 by 3,000
    C.   divide 800 by 30
    D.   multiply 30 by the fraction 2,200 divided by 3,000

9. Six gross of special drawing pencils were purchased for use in a city department.   9._____
If the pencils were used at the rate of 24 a week, the MAXIMUM number of weeks that
the six gross of pencils would last is _____ weeks.

    A. 6   B. 12   C. 24   D. 36

10. A stock clerk had 600 pads on hand. He then issued 3/8 of his supply of pads to Division   10._____
X, 1/4 to Division Y, and 1/6 to Division Z.
The number of pads remaining in stock is

    A. 48   B. 125   C. 240   D. 475

11. If a certain job can be performed by 18 clerks in 26 days, the number of clerks needed to   11._____
perform the job in 12 days is _____ clerks.

    A. 24   B. 30   C. 39   D. 52

12. In anticipation of a seasonal increase in the amount of work to be performed by his divi-   12._____
sion, a division chief prepared the following list of additional temporary employees
needed by his division and the amount of time they would be employed:
    26 cashiers, each at $24,000 a year, for 2 months
    15 laborers, each at $85.00 a day, for 50 days
    6 clerks, each at $21,000 a year, for 3 months
The total approximate cost for this additional personnel would be MOST NEARLY

    A. $200,000   B. $250,000   C. $500,000   D. $600,000

13. A copy machine company offered to sell a city agency 4 copy machines at a discount of   13._____
15% from the list price, and to allow the agency $850 for each of its two old machines.
The list price of the new machines is $6,250 per machine.
If the city agency accepts this offer, the amount of money it will have to provide for the
purchase of these 4 machines is

    A. $17,350   B. $22,950   C. $19,550   D. $18,360

14. A stationery buyer was offered bond paper at the following price scale:
    $1.43 per ream for the first 1,000 reams
    $1.30 per ream for the next 4,000 reams
    $1.20 per ream for each additional ream beyond 5,000 reams
    If the buyer ordered 10,000 reams of paper, the average cost per ream, computed to
    the nearest cent, was

    A. $1.24   B. $1.26   C. $1.31   D. $1.36

15. A clerk has 5.70 percent of his salary deducted for his retirement pension.
    If this clerk's annual salary is $20,400, the monthly deduction for his retirement pen-
    sion is

    A. $298.20   B. $357.90   C. $1,162.80   D. $96.90

16. In a certain bureau, two-thirds of the employees are clerks and the remainder are typists.
    If there are 90 clerks, then the number of typists in this bureau is

    A. 135   B. 45   C. 120   D. 30

17. The number of investigations conducted by an agency in 1999 was 3,600. In 2000, the
    number of investigations conducted was one-third more than in 1999. The number of
    investigations conducted in 2001 was three-fourths of the number conducted in 2000. It
    is anticipated that the number of investigations conducted in 2002 will be equal to the
    average of the three preceding years. On the basis of this information, the MOST accu-
    rate of the following statements is that the number of investigations conducted in

    A. 1999 is larger than the number anticipated for 2002
    B. 2000 is smaller than the number anticipated for 2002
    C. 2001 is equal to the number conducted in 1999
    D. 2001 is larger than the number anticipated in 2002

18. A city agency engaged in repair work uses a small part which the city purchases for 14
    each. Assume that, in a certain year, the total expenditure of the city for this part was
    $700.
    How many of these parts were purchased that year?

    A. 50   B. 200   C. 2,000   D. 5,000

19. The work unit which you supervise is responsible for processing 15 reports per month.
    If your unit has 4 clerks and the best worker completes 40% of the reports himself, how
    many reports would each of the other clerks have to complete if they all do an equal
    number?

    A. 1   B. 2   C. 3   D. 4

14.__

15.__

16.__

17.__

18.__

19.__

20. Assume that the work unit in which you work has 24 clerks and 18 stenographers. In order to change the ratio of stenographers to clerks so that there is 1 stenographer for every 4 clerks, it would be necessary to REDUCE the number of stenographers by

    A. 3   B. 6   C. 9   D. 12

    20.____

21. The arithmetic mean salary for five employees earning $18,500, $18,300, $18,600, $18,400, and $18,500, respectively, is

    A. $18,450   B. $18,460   C. $18,475   D. $18,500

    21.____

22. Last year, a city department which is responsible for purchasing supplies ordered bond paper in equal quantities from 22 different companies. The price was exactly the same for each company, and the total cost for the 22 orders was $693,113.
    Assuming prices did not change during the year, the cost of each order was MOST NEARLY

    A. $31,490   B. $31,495   C. $31,500   D. $31,505

    22.____

23. Suppose that a large bureau has 187 employees. On a particular day, approximately 14% of these employees are not available for work because of absences due to vacation, illness, or other reasons. Of the remaining employees, 1/7 are assigned to a special project while the balance are assigned to the normal work of the bureau. The number of employees assigned to the normal work of the bureau on that day is

    A. 112   B. 124   C. 138   D. 142

    23.____

24. Suppose that you are in charge of a typing pool of 8 typists. Two typists type at the rate of 38 words per minute; three type at the rate of 40 words per minute; three type at the rate of 42 words per minute. The average typewritten page consists of 50 lines, 12 words per line. Each employee works from 9 to 5 with one hour off for lunch.
    The total number of pages typed by this pool in one day is, on the average, CLOSEST to _____ pages.

    A. 205   B. 225   C. 250   D. 275

    24.____

25. Suppose that part-time workers are paid $7.20 an hour, prorated to the nearest half hour, with pay guaranteed for a minimum of four hours if services are required for less than four hours. In one operation, part-time workers signed the time sheet as follows:

Worker	In		Out	
A	8:00	A.M.	11:35	A.M.
B	8:30	A.M.	3:20	P.M.
C	7:55	A.M.	11:00	A.M.
D	8:30	A.M.	2:25	P.M.

    How much would TOTAL payment to these part-time workers amount to for this operation, assuming that those who stayed after 12 Noon were not paid for one hour which they took off for lunch?

    A. $134.40   B. $136.80   C. $142.20   D. $148.80

    25.____

KEY (CORRECT ANSWERS)

1.	C	11.	C
2.	C	12.	A
3.	C	13.	C
4.	B	14.	B
5.	D	15.	D
6.	B	16.	B
7.	C	17.	C
8.	C	18.	D
9.	D	19.	C
10.	B	20.	D

21.	B
22.	D
23.	C
24.	B
25.	B

SOLUTIONS TO PROBLEMS

1. Maximum number of folders = (4)(12)(20) = 960

2. (3500+6700+10,500)(.95) = 19,665

3. Hourly rate = \$18,928 ÷ 1820 = \$10.40. Then, the pay for 18 hours = (\$10.40)(18) = \$187.20

4. Total pay = (\$11.20)(40) + (\$11.20)(1.5)(3) = \$498.40

5. (1 - 1/5 - 1/2 - 1/7)(100)% ≈ 16%

6. Previous cost for five years = (\$324,000)(5) = \$1,620,000
   Present cost for five years = (5)(5)(\$1,400) + (5)(5)(\$100) + (5)(5)(\$30,000) + (1)(5)(\$38,000) = \$977,500   The net savings = \$642,500 ≈ \$640,000

7. (12)(18) = 216 clerk-days. Then, 216 - (12)(6) = 144 clerk-days of work left when 4 more clerks are added. Now, 16 clerks will finish the task in 144 ÷ 16 = 9 more days. Finally, the task will require a total of 6 + 9 = 15 days.

8. Number of days needed = (3000-2200) ÷ 30 = 26.7, which is equivalent to dividing 800 by 30.

9. (6)(144) = 864 pencils purchased. Then, 864 ÷ 24 = 36 maximum number of weeks

10. Number of remaining pads = 600 - (1)(600) - (1/4)(600) - (1/6)(600) = 125

11. (18)(26) ÷ 12 = 39 clerks

12. Total cost = (26)(\$24,000)(2/12) + (15)(\$85)(50) + (6)(\$21,000)(3/12) = \$199,250
    \$200,000

13. (4)(\$6250)(.85) - (2)(\$850) = \$19,550

14. Total cost = (\$1.43)(1000) + (\$1.30)(4000) + (\$1.20X5000) = \$12,630. Average cost per ream = \$12,630 10,000 ≈ \$1.26

15. Monthly salary = \$20,400 ÷ 12 = \$1700. Thus, the monthly deduction for his pension = (\$1700)(.057) + \$96.90

16. Number of employees = 90 ÷ 2/3 = 135. Then, the number of typists = (1/3)(135) = 45

17. The number of investigations for each year is as follows:
    1999: 3600
    2000: (3600)(1 1/3) = 4800
    2001: (4800)(3/4) = 3600
    2002: (3600+4800+3600)/3 = 4000
    So, the number of investigations were equal for 1999 and 2001.

18. \$700 ÷ .14 = 5000 parts

19. The best worker does (.40)(15) = 6 reports. The other 9 reports are divided equally among the other 3 clerks, so each clerk does 9 ÷ 3 = 3 reports.

20. 1:4 = 6:24 . Thus, the number of stenographers must be reduced by 18 - 6 = 12

21. Mean = ($18,500+$18,300+$18,400+$18,500) ÷ 5 = $18,460

22. The cost per order = $693,113 ÷ 22 ≈ $31,505

23. 187 - (.14) = 26. 187 - 26 = 161 - 1/7 (161) = 23
    161 - 23 = 138

24. Number of words typed in 1 min. = (2)(38) + (3)(40) + (3)(42) = 322. For 7 hours, the total number of words typed = (7)(60)(322) = 135,240. Each page contains (on the average) (50)(12) = 600 words. Finally, 135,240 ÷ 600 ≈ 225 pages

25. Worker A = ($7.20)(4) = $28.80
    Worker B = ($7.20)(3 1/2) + ($7.20)(2 1/2) = $43.20
    Worker C = ($7.20)(4) = $28.80
    Worker D = ($7.20)(3 1/2) + ($7.20)(1 1/2) = $36.00
    Total for all 4 workers = $136.80
    Note: Workers A and C received the guaranteed minimum 4 hours pay each.

READING COMPREHENSION
UNDERSTANDING AND INTERPRETING WRITTEN MATERIAL
EXAMINATION SECTION
TEST 1

DIRECTIONS: Each question or incomplete statement is followed by several suggested answers or completions. Select the one that BEST answers the question or completes the statement. *PRINT THE LETTER OF THE CORRECT ANSWER IN THE SPACE AT THE RIGHT.*

Questions 1-2.

DIRECTIONS: Questions 1 and 2 are to be answered SOLELY on the basis of the following passage.

The employees in a unit or division of a government agency may be referred to as a work group. Within a government agency which has existed for some time, the work groups will have evolved traditions of their own. The persons in these work groups acquire these traditions as part of the process of work adjustment within their groups. Usually, a work group in a large organization will contain *oldtimers*, *newcomers*, and *in-betweeners*. Like the supervisor of a group, who is not necessarily an oldtimer or the oldest member, oldtimers usually have great influence. They can recall events unknown to others and are a storehouse of information and advice about current problems in the light of past experience. They pass along the traditions of the group to the others who, in turn, become oldtimers themselves. Thus, the traditions of the group which have been honored and revered by long acceptance are continued.

1.   According to the above passage, the traditions of a work group within a government agency are developed

    A.   at the time the group is established
    B.   over a considerable period of time
    C.   in order to give recognition to oldtimers
    D.   for the group before it is established

1.____

2.   According to the above passage, the oldtimers within a work group

    A.   are the means by which long accepted practices and customs are perpetuated
    B.   would best be able to settle current problems that arise
    C.   are honored because of the changes they have made in the traditions
    D.   have demonstrated that they have learned to do their work well

2.____

Questions 3-4.

DIRECTIONS: Questions 3 and 4 are to be answered SOLELY on the basis of the following passage.

In public agencies, the success of a person assigned to perform first-line supervisory duties depends in large part upon the personal relations between him and his subordinate employees. The goal of supervising effort is something more than to obtain compliance with procedures established by some central office. The major objective is work accomplishment. In order for this goal to be attained, employees must want to attain it and must exercise initiative in their work. Only if employees are generally satisfied with the type of supervision which exists in an organization will they put forth their best efforts.

3. According to the above passage, in order for employees to try to do their work as well as they can, it is essential that

    A.   they participate in determining their working conditions and rates of pay
    B.   their supervisors support the employees' viewpoints in meetings with higher management
    C.   they are content with the supervisory practices which are being used
    D.   their supervisors make the changes in working procedures that the employees request

4. It can be inferred from the above passage that the goals of a unit in a public agency will not be reached unless the employees in the unit

    A.   wish to reach them and are given the opportunity to make individual contributions to the work
    B.   understand the relationship between the goals of the unit and goals of the agency
    C.   have satisfactory personal relationships with employees of other units in the agency
    D.   carefully follow the directions issued by higher authorities

Questions 5-9.

DIRECTIONS: Questions 5 through 9 are to be answered SOLELY on the basis of the following passage.

If an employee thinks he can save money, time, or material for the city or has an idea about how to do something better than it is being done, he shouldn't keep it to himself. He should send his ideas to the Employees' Suggestion Program, using the special form which is kept on hand in all departments. An employee may send in as many ideas as he wishes. To make sure that each idea is judged fairly, the name of the suggester is not made known until an award is made. The awards are certificates of merit or cash prizes ranging from $10 to $500.

5. According to the above passage, an employee who knows how to do a job in a better way should

    A.   be sure it saves enough time to be worthwhile
    B.   get paid the money he saves for the city
    C.   keep it to himself to avoid being accused of causing a speed-up
    D.   send his idea to the Employees' Suggestion Program

6. In order to send his idea to the Employees' Suggestion Program, an employee should   6._____

    A. ask the Department of Personnel for a special form
    B. get the special form in his own department
    C. mail the idea using Special Delivery
    D. send it on plain, white letter-size paper

7. An employee may send to the Employees' Suggestion Program   7._____

    A. as many ideas as he can think of
    B. no more than one idea each week
    C. no more than ten ideas in a month
    D. only one idea on each part of the job

8. The reason the name of an employee who makes a suggestion is not made known at first is to   8._____

    A. give the employee a larger award
    B. help the judges give more awards
    C. insure fairness in judging
    D. only one idea on each part of the job

9. An employee whose suggestion receives an award may be given a   9._____

    A. bonus once a year
    B. certificate for $10
    C. cash prize of up to $500
    D. salary increase of $500

Questions 10-12.

DIRECTIONS: Questions 10 through 12 are to be answered SOLELY on the basis of the following passage.

According to the rules of the Department of Personnel, the work of every permanent city employee is reviewed and rated by his supervisor at least once a year. The civil service rating system gives the employee and his supervisor a chance to talk about the progress made during the past year as well as about those parts of the job in which the employee needs to do better. In order to receive a pay increase each year, the employee must have a satisfactory service rating. Service ratings also count toward an employee's final mark on a promotion examination.

10. According to the above passage, a permanent city employee is rated AT LEAST once   10._____

    A. before his work is reviewed
    B. every six months
    C. yearly by his supervisor
    D. yearly by the Department of Personnel

11. According to the above passage, under the rating system the supervisor and the employee can discuss how   11._____

    A. much more work needs to be done next year
    B. the employee did his work last year

C. the work can be made easier next year
D. the work of the Department can be increased

12. According to the above passage, a permanent city employee will NOT receive a yearly   12._
pay increase

A. if he received a pay increase the year before
B. if he used his service rating for his mark on a promotion examination
C. if his service rating is unsatisfactory
D. unless he got some kind of a service rating

Questions 13-16.

DIRECTIONS: Questions 13 through 16 are to be answered SOLELY on the basis of the
following passage.

It is an accepted fact that the rank and file employee can frequently advance worthwhile
suggestions toward increasing efficiency. For this reason, an Employees' Suggestion System
has been developed and put into operation. Suitable means have been provided at each
departmental location for the confidential submission of suggestions. Numerous suggestions
have been received thus far and, after study, about five percent of the ideas submitted are
being translated into action. It is planned to set up, eventually, monetary awards for all worthwhile suggestions.

13. According to the above passage, a MAJOR reason why an Employees' Suggestion Sys-   13._
tem was established is that

A. an organized program of improvement is better than a haphazard one
B. employees can often give good suggestions to increase efficiency
C. once a fact is accepted, it is better to act on it than to do nothing
D. the suggestions of rank and file employees were being neglected

14. According to the above passage, under the Employees' Suggestion System,   14._

A. a file of worthwhile suggestions will eventually be set up at each departmental
location
B. it is possible for employees to turn in suggestions without fellow employees knowing of it
C. means have been provided for the regular and frequent collection of suggestions
submitted
D. provision has been made for the judging of worthwhile suggestions by an Employees' Suggestion Committee

15. According to the above passage, it is reasonable to assume that   15._

A. all suggestions must be turned in at a central office
B. employees who make worthwhile suggestions will be promoted
C. not all the prizes offered will be monetary ones
D. prizes of money will be given for the best suggestions

16. According to the above passage, of the many suggestions made,   16._____

    A. all are first tested
    B. a small part are put into use
    C. most are very worthwhile
    D. samples are studied

Questions 17-20.

DIRECTIONS: Questions 17 through 20 are to be answered SOLELY on the basis of the following passage.

Employees may be granted leaves of absence without pay at the discretion of the Personnel Officer. Such a leave without pay shall begin on the first working day on which the employee does not report for duty and shall continue to the first day on which the employee returns to duty. The Personnel Division may vary the dates of the leave for the record so as to conform with payroll periods, but in no case shall an employee be off the payroll for a different number of calendar days than would have been the case if the actual dates mentioned above had been used. An employee who has vacation or overtime to his credit, which is available for normal use, may take time off immediately prior to beginning a leave of absence without pay, chargeable against all or part of such vacation or overtime.

17. According to the above passage, the Personnel Officer must   17._____

    A. decide if a leave of absence without pay should be granted
    B. require that a leave end on the last working day of a payroll period
    C. see to it that a leave of absence begins on the first working day of a pay period
    D. vary the dates of a leave of absence to conform with a payroll period

18. According to the above passage, the exact dates of a leave of absence without pay may   18._____
be varied provided that the

    A. calendar days an employee is off the payroll equal the actual leave granted
    B. leave conforms to an even number of payroll periods
    C. leave when granted made provision for variance to simplify payroll records
    D. Personnel Officer approves the variation

19. According to the above passage, a leave of absence without pay must extend from the   19._____

    A. first day of a calendar period to the first day the employee resumes work
    B. first day of a payroll period to the last calendar day of the leave
    C. first working day missed to the first day on which the employee resumes work
    D. last day on which an employee works through the first day he returns to work

20. According to the above passage, an employee may take extra time off just before the   20._____
start of a leave of absence without pay if

    A. he charges this extra time against his leave
    B. he has a favorable balance of vacation or overtime which has been frozen
    C. the vacation or overtime that he would normally use for a leave without pay has not
       been charged in this way before
    D. there is time to his credit which he may use

Question 21.

DIRECTIONS: Question 21 is to be answered SOLELY on the basis of the following passage.

In considering those things which are motivators and incentives to work, it might be just as erroneous not to give sufficient weight to money as an incentive as it is to give too much weight. It is not a problem of establishing a rank-order of importance, but one of knowing that motivation is a blend or mixture rather than a pure element. It is simple to say that cultural factors count more than financial considerations, but this leads only to the conclusion that our society is financial-oriented.

21.   Based on the above passage, in our society, cultural and social motivations to work are   21.____

    A.   things which cannot be avoided
    B.   melded to financial incentives
    C.   of less consideration than high pay
    D.   not balanced equally with economic or financial considerations

Question 22.

DIRECTIONS: Question 22 is to be answered SOLELY on the basis of the following passage.

A general principle of training and learning with respect to people is that they learn more readily if they receive *feedback*. Essential to maintaining proper motivational levels is knowledge of results which indicate level of progress. Feedback also assists the learning process by identifying mistakes. If this kind of information were not given to the learner, then improper or inappropriate job performance may be instilled.

22.   Based on the above passage, which of the following is MOST accurate?   22.____

    A.   Learning will not take place without feedback.
    B.   In the absence of feedback, improper or inappropriate job performance will be learned.
    C.   To properly motivate a learner, the learner must have his progress made known to him.
    D.   Trainees should be told exactly what to do if they are to learn properly.

Question 23.

DIRECTIONS: Question 23 is to be answered SOLELY on the basis of the following passage.

In a democracy, the obligation of public officials is twofold. They must not only do an efficient and satisfactory job of administration, but also they must persuade the public that it is an efficient and satisfactory job. It is a burden which, if properly assumed, will make democracy work and perpetuate reform government.

23.   The above passage means that   23.____

    A.   public officials should try to please everybody
    B.   public opinion is instrumental in determining the policy of public officials

C. satisfactory performance of the job of administration will eliminate opposition to its work
D. frank and open procedure in a public agency will aid in maintaining progressive government

Question 24.

DIRECTIONS: Question 24 is to be answered SOLELY on the basis of the following passage.

Upon retirement for service, a member shall receive a retirement allowance which shall consist of an annuity which shall be the actuarial equivalent of his accumulated deductions at the time of his retirement and a pension, in addition to his annuity, which shall be equal to one service-fraction of his final compensation, multiplied by the number of years of service since he last became a member credited to him, and a pension which is the actuarial equivalent of the reserve-for-increased-take-home-pay to which he may then be entitled, if any.

24. According to the above passage, a retirement allowance shall consist of a(n)   24.____

   A. annuity, plus a pension, plus an actuarial equivalent
   B. annuity, plus a pension, plus reserve-for-increased-take-home-pay, if any
   C. annuity, plus reserve-for-increased-take-home-pay, if any, plus final compensation
   D. pension, plus reserve-for-increased-take-home-pay, if any, plus accumulated deductions

Question 25.

DIRECTIONS: Question 25 is to be answered SOLELY on the basis of the following passage.

Membership in the retirement system shall cease upon the occurrence of any one of the following conditions: when the time out of service of any member who has total service of less than 25 years, shall aggregate more than 5 years; when the time out of service of any member who has total service of 25 years or more, shall aggregate more than 10 years; when any member shall have withdrawn more than 50% of his accumulated deductions; or when any member shall have withdrawn the cash benefit provided by Section B3-35.0 of the Administrative Code.

25. According to the information in the above passage, membership in the retirement system   25.____
    shall cease when an employee

   A. with 17 years of service has been on a leave of absence for 3 years
   B. withdraws 50% of his accumulated deductions
   C. with 28 years of service has been out of service for 10 years
   D. withdraws his cash benefits

KEY (CORRECT ANSWERS)

1.	B		11.	B
2.	A		12.	C
3.	C		13.	B
4.	A		14.	B
5.	D		15.	D
6.	B		16.	B
7.	A		17.	A
8.	C		18.	A
9.	B		19.	C
10.	C		20.	D

21.	B
22.	C
23.	D
24.	B
25.	D

———

TEST 2

DIRECTIONS: Each question or incomplete statement is followed by several suggested answers or completions. Select the one that BEST answers the question or completes the statement. *PRINT THE LETTER OF THE CORRECT ANSWER IN THE SPACE AT THE RIGHT.*

Questions 1-6.

DIRECTIONS: Questions 1 through 6 are to be answered SOLELY on the basis of the following passage from an old office manual.

Since almost every office has some contact with data-processed records, a stenographer should have some understanding of the basic operations of data processing. Data processing systems now handle about one-third of all office paperwork. On punched cards, magnetic tape, or on other mediums, data are recorded before being fed into the computer for processing. A machine such as the keypunch is used to convert the data written on the source document into the coded symbols on punched cards or tapes. After data has been converted, it must be verified to guarantee absolute accuracy of conversion. In this manner, data becomes a permanent record which can be read by electronic computers that compare, store, compute, and otherwise process data at high speeds.

One key person in a computer installation is a programmer, the man or woman who puts business and scientific problems into special symbolic languages that can be read by the computer. Jobs done by the computer range all the way from payroll operations to chemical process control, but most computer applications are directed toward management data. About half of the programmers employed by business come to their positions with college degrees; the remaining half are promoted to their positions from within the organization on the basis of demonstrated ability without regard to education.

1. Of the following, the BEST title for the above passage is   1.____

   A. THE STENOGRAPHER AS DATA PROCESSOR
   B. THE RELATION OF KEYPUNCHING TO STENOGRAPHY
   C. UNDERSTANDING DATA PROCESSING
   D. PERMANENT OFFICE RECORDS

2. According to the above passage, a stenographer should understand the basic operations   2.____
   of data processing because

   A. almost every office today has contact with data processed by computer
   B. any office worker may be asked to verify the accuracy of data
   C. most offices are involved in the production of permanent records
   D. data may be converted into computer language by typing on a keypunch

3. According to the above passage, the data which the computer understands is MOST   3.____
   often expressed as

   A. a scientific programming language
   B. records or symbols punched on tape, cards, or other mediums
   C. records on cards
   D. records on tape

4. According to the above passage, computers are used MOST often to handle   4.___

   A. management data
   B. problems of higher education
   C. the control of chemical processes
   D. payroll operations

5. Computer programming is taught in many colleges and business schools.   5.___
The above passage implies that programmers in industry

   A. must have professional training
   B. need professional training to advance
   C. must have at least a college education to do adequate programming tasks
   D. do not need college education to do programming work

6. According to the above passage, data to be processed by computer should be   6.___

   A. recent   B. basic
   C. complete   D. verified

Questions 7-10.

DIRECTIONS: Questions 7 through 10 are to be answered SOLELY on the basis of the following passage.

There is nothing that will take the place of good sense on the part of the stenographer. You may be perfect in transcribing exactly what the dictator says and your speed may be adequate, but without an understanding of the dictator's intent as well as his words, you are likely to be a mediocre secretary.

A serious error that is made when taking dictation is putting down something that does not make sense. Most people who dictate material would rather be asked to repeat and explain than to receive transcribed material which has errors due to inattention or doubt. Many dictators request that their grammar be corrected by their secretaries, but unless specifically asked to do so, secretaries should not do it without first checking with the dictator. Secretaries should be aware that, in some cases, dictators may use incorrect grammar or slang expressions to create a particular effect.

Some people dictate commas, periods, and paragraphs, while others expect the stenographer to know when, where, and how to punctuate. A well-trained secretary should be able to indicate the proper punctuation by listening to the pauses and tones of the dictator's voice.

A stenographer who has taken dictation from the same person for a period of time should be able to understand him under most conditions, By increasing her tact, alertness, and efficiency, a secretary can become more competent.

7. According to the above passage, which of the following statements concerning the dictation of punctuation is CORRECT?   7.___

   A. Dictator may use incorrect punctuation to create a desired style
   B. Dictator should indicate all punctuation
   C. Stenographer should know how to punctuate based on the pauses and tones of the dictator
   D. Stenographer should not type any punctuation if it has not been dictated to her

8. According to the above passage, how should secretaries handle grammatical errors in a dictation? Secretaries should

    A. *not correct* grammatical errors unless the dictator is aware that this is being done
    B. *correct* grammatical errors by having the dictator repeat the line with proper pauses
    C. *correct* grammatical errors if they have checked the correctness in a grammar book
    D. *correct* grammatical errors based on their own good sense

8._____

9. If a stenographer is confused about the method of spacing and indenting of a report which has just been dictated to her, she GENERALLY should

    A. do the best she can
    B. ask the dictator to explain what she should do
    C. try to improve her ability to understand dictated material
    D. accept the fact that her stenographic ability is not adequate

9._____

10. In the last line of the first paragraph, the word *mediocre* means MOST NEARLY

    A. superior
    B. respected
    C. disregarded
    D. second-rate

10._____

Questions 11-12.

DIRECTIONS: Questions 11 and 12 are to be answered SOLELY on the basis of the following passage.

The number of legible carbon copies required to be produced determines the weight of the carbon paper to be used. When only one copy is made, heavy carbon paper is satisfactory. Most typists, however, use medium-weight carbon paper and find it serviceable for up to three or four copies. If five or more copies are to be made, it is wise to use light carbon paper. On the other hand, the finish of carbon paper to be used depends largely on the stroke of the typist and, in lesser degree, on the number of copies to be made and on whether the typewriter has pica or elite type. A soft-finish carbon paper should be used if the typist's touch is light or if a noiseless machine is used. It is desirable for the average typist to use medium-finish carbon paper for ordinary work, when only a few carbon copies are required. Elite type requires a harder carbon finish than pica type for the same number of copies.

11. According to the above passage, the lighter the carbon paper used,

    A. the softer the finish of the carbon paper will be
    B. the greater the number of legible carbon copies that can be made
    C. the greater the number of times the carbon paper can be used
    D. the lighter the typist's touch should be

11._____

12. According to the above passage, the MOST important factor which determines whether the finish of carbon paper to be used in typing should be hard, medium, or soft is

    A. the touch of the typist
    B. the number of carbon copies required
    C. whether the type in the typewriter is pica or elite
    D. whether a machine with pica type will produce the same number of carbon copies as a machine with elite type

12._____

Questions 13-16.

DIRECTIONS: Questions 13 through 16 are to be answered SOLELY on the basis of the following passage.

Modern office methods, geared to ever higher speeds and aimed at ever greater efficiency, are largely the result of the typewriter. The typewriter is a substitute for handwriting and, in the hands of a skilled typist, not only turns out letters and other documents at least three times faster than a penman can do the work, but turns out the greater volume more uniformly and legibly. With the use of carbon paper and onionskin paper, identical copies can be made at the same time.

The typewriter, besides its effect on the conduct of business and government, has had a very important effect on the position of women. The typewriter has done much to bring women into business and government, and today there are vastly more women than men typists. Many women have used the keys of the typewriter to climb the ladder to responsible managerial positions.

The typewriter, as its name implies, employs type to make an ink impression on paper. For many years, the manual typewriter was the standard machine used. Today, the electric typewriter is dominant, and completely automatic electronic typewriters are coming into wider use.

The mechanism of the office manual typewriter includes a set of keys arranged systematically in rows; a semicircular frame of type, connected to the keys by levers; the carriage, or paper carrier; a rubber roller, called a platen, against which the type strikes; and an inked ribbon which make the impression of the type character when the key strikes it.

13. The above passage mentions a number of good features of the combination of a skilled typist and a typewriter. Of the following, the feature which is NOT mentioned in the passage is   13.___

   A. speed   B. reliability
   C. uniformity   D. legibility

14. According to the above passage, a skilled typist can   14.___

   A. turn out at least five carbon copies of typed matter
   B. type at least three times faster than a penman can write
   C. type more than 80 words a minute
   D. readily move into a managerial position

15. According to the above passage, which of the following is NOT part of the mechanism of   15.___
   a manual typewriter?

   A. Carbon paper   B. Platen
   C. Paper carrier   D. Inked ribbon

16. According to the above passage, the typewriter has helped   16.___

   A. men more than women in business
   B. women in career advancement into management
   C. men and women equally, but women have taken better advantage of it
   D. more women than men, because men generally dislike routine typing work

Questions 17-21.

DIRECTIONS: Questions 17 through 21 are to be answered SOLELY on the basis of the following passage.

The recipient gains an impression of a typewritten letter before he begins to read the message. Factors which provide for a good first impression include margins and spacing that are visually pleasing, formal parts of the letter which are correctly placed according to the style of the letter, copy which is free of obvious erasures and over-strikes, and transcript that is even and clear. The problem for the typist is that of how to produce that first, positive impression of her work.

There are several general rules which a typist can follow when she wishes to prepare a properly spaced letter on a sheet of letterhead. Ordinarily, the width of a letter should not be less than four inches nor more than six inches. The side margins should also have a desirable relation to the bottom margin and the space between the letterhead and the body of the letter. Usually the most appealing arrangement is when the side margins are even and the bottom margin is slightly wider than the side margins. In some offices, however, standard line length is used for all business letters, and the secretary then varies the spacing between the date line and the inside address according to the length of the letter.

17. The BEST title for the above passage would be   17._____

    A. WRITING OFFICE LETTERS
    B. MAKING GOOD FIRST IMPRESSIONS
    C. JUDGING WELL-TYPED LETTERS
    D. GOOD PLACING AND SPACING FOR OFFICE LETTERS

18. According to the above passage, which of the following might be considered the way in   18._____
    which people very quickly judge the quality of work which has been typed? By

    A. measuring the margins to see if they are correct
    B. looking at the spacing and cleanliness of the typescript
    C. scanning the body of the letter for meaning
    D. reading the date line and address for errors

19. What, according to the above passage, would be definitely UNDESIRABLE as the aver-   19._____
    age line length of a typed letter?

    A. 4"   B. 6"
    C. 5"   D. 7"

20. According to the above passage, when the line length is kept standard, the secretary   20._____

    A. does not have to vary the spacing at all since this also is standard
    B. adjusts the spacing between the date line and inside address for different lengths
        of letters
    C. uses the longest line as a guideline for spacing between the date line and inside
        address
    D. varies-the number of spaces between the lines

21. According to the above passage, side margins are MOST pleasing when they   21.___

    A. are even and somewhat smaller than the bottom margin
    B. are slightly wider than the bottom margin
    C. vary with the length of the letter
    D. are figured independently from the letterhead and the body of the letter

Questions 22-25.

DIRECTIONS: Questions 22 through 25 are to be answered SOLELY on the basis of the following passage.

Typed pages can reflect the simplicity of modern art in a machine age. Lightness and evenness can be achieved by proper layout and balance of typed lines and white space. Instead of solid, cramped masses of uneven, crowded typing, there should be a pleasing balance up and down as well as horizontal.

To have real balance, your page must have a center. The eyes see the center of the sheet slightly above the real center. This is the way both you and the reader see it. Try imagining a line down the center of the page that divides the paper in equal halves. On either side of your paper, white space and blocks of typing need to be similar in size and shape. Although left and right margins should be equal, top and bottom margins need not be as exact. It looks better to hold a bottom border wider than a top margin, so that your typing rests upon a cushion of white space. To add interest to the appearance of the page, try making one paragraph between one-half and two-thirds the size of an adjacent paragraph.

Thus, by taking full advantage of your typewriter, the pages that you type will not only be accurate but will also be attractive.

22. It can be inferred from the above passage that the basic importance of proper balancing   22.___
    on a typed page is that proper balancing

    A. makes a typed page a work of modern art
    B. provides exercise in proper positioning of a typewriter
    C. increases the amount of typed copy on the paper
    D. draws greater attention and interest to the page

23. A reader will tend to see the center of a typed page   23.___

    A. somewhat higher than the true center
    B. somewhat lower than the true center
    C. on either side of the true center
    D. about two-thirds of an inch above the true center

24. Which of the following suggestions is NOT given by the above passage?   24.___

    A. Bottom margins may be wider than top borders.
    B. Keep all paragraphs approximately the same size.
    C. Divide your page with an imaginary line down the middle.
    D. Side margins should be equalized.

25. Of the following, the BEST title for the above passage is   25.____

    A. INCREASING THE ACCURACY OF THE TYPED PAGE
    B. DETERMINATION OF MARGINS FOR TYPED COPY
    C. LAYOUT AND BALANCE OF THE TYPED PAGE
    D. HOW TO TAKE FULL ADVANTAGE OF THE TYPEWRITER

KEY (CORRECT ANSWERS)

1.	C		11.	B
2.	A		12.	A
3.	B		13.	C
4.	A		14.	B
5.	D		15.	A
6.	D		16.	B
7.	C		17.	D
8.	A		18.	B
9.	B		19.	D
10.	D		20.	B

21.	A
22.	D
23.	A
24.	B
25.	C

TEST 3

Questions 1-5.

DIRECTIONS: Questions 1 through 5 are to be answered SOLELY on the basis of the following passage.

A written report is a communication of information from one person to another. It is an account of some matter especially investigated, however routine that matter may be. The ultimate basis of any good written report is facts, which become known through observation and verification. Good written reports may seem to be no more than general ideas and opinions. However, in such cases, the facts leading to these opinions were gathered, verified, and reported earlier, and the opinions are dependent upon these facts. Good style, proper form, and emphasis cannot make a good written report out of unreliable information and bad judgment; but on the other hand, solid investigation and brilliant thinking are not likely to become very useful until they are effectively communicated to others. If a person's work calls for written reports, then his work is often no better than his written reports.

1. Based on the information in the above passage, it can be concluded that opinions expressed in a report should be   1.

   A. based on facts which are gathered and reported
   B. emphasized repeatedly when they result from a special investigation
   C. kept to a minimum
   D. separated from the body of the report

2. In the above passage, the one of the following which is mentioned as a way of establishing facts is   2.

   A. authority   B. reporting
   C. communication   D. verification

3. According to the above passage, the characteristic shared by ALL written reports is that they are   3.

   A. accounts of routine matters   B. transmissions of information
   C. reliable and logical   D. written in proper form

4. Which of the following conclusions can logically be drawn from the information given in the above passage?   4.

   A. Brilliant thinking can make up for unreliable information in a report.
   B. One method of judging an individual's work is the quality of the written reports he is required to submit.
   C. Proper form and emphasis can make a good report out of unreliable information.
   D. Good written reports that seem to be no more than general ideas should be rewritten.

5. Which of the following suggested titles would be MOST appropriate for the above pas-   5.___
   sage?

    A. GATHERING AND ORGANIZING FACTS
    B. TECHNIQUES OF OBSERVATION
    C. NATURE AND PURPOSE OF REPORTS
    D. REPORTS AND OPINIONS: DIFFERENCES AND SIMILARITIES

Questions 6-8.

DIRECTIONS: Questions 6 through 8 are to be answered SOLELY on the basis of the following passage.

    The most important unit of the mimeograph machine is a perforated metal drum over which is stretched a cloth ink pad. A reservoir inside the drum contains the ink which flows through the perforations and saturates the ink pad. To operate the machine, the operator first removes from the machine the protective sheet, which keeps the ink from drying while the machine is not in use. He then hooks the stencil face down on the drum, draws the stencil smoothly over the drum, and fastens the stencil at the bottom. The speed with which the drum turns determines the blackness of the copies printed. Slow turning gives heavy, black copies; fast turning gives light, clear-cut reproductions. If reproductions are run on other than porous paper, slip-sheeting is necessary to prevent smearing. Often, the printed copy fails to drop readily as it comes from the machine. This may be due to static electricity. To remedy this difficulty, the operator fastens a strip of tinsel from side to side near the impression roller so that the printed copy just touches the soft stems of the tinsel as it is ejected from the machine, thus grounding the static electricity to the frame of the machine.

6. According to the above passage,   6.___

    A. turning the drum fast produces light copies
    B. stencils should be placed face up on the drum
    C. ink pads should be changed daily
    D. slip-sheeting is necessary when porous paper is being used

7. According to the above passage, when a mimeograph machine is not in use,   7.___

    A. the ink should be drained from the drum
    B. the ink pad should be removed
    C. the machine should be covered with a protective sheet
    D. the counter should be set at zero

8. According to the above passage, static electricity is grounded to the frame of the mimeo-   8.___
   graph machine by means of

    A. a slip-sheeting device
    B. a strip of tinsel
    C. an impression roller
    D. hooks located at the top of the drum

Questions 9-10.

DIRECTIONS: Questions 9 and 10 are to be answered SOLELY on the basis of the following passage.

The proofreading of material typed from copy is performed more accurately and more speedily when two persons perform this work as a team. The person who did not do the typing should read aloud the original copy while the person who did the typing should check the reading against the typed copy. The reader should speak very slowly and repeat the figures, using a different grouping of numbers when repeating the figures. For example, in reading 1967, the reader may say *one-nine-six-seven* on first reading the figure and *nineteen-sixty-seven* on repeating the figure. The reader should read all punctuation marks, taking nothing for granted. Since mistakes can occur anywhere, everything typed should be proofread. To avoid confusion, the proofreading team should use the standard proofreading marks, which are given in most dictionaries.

9. According to the above passage, the

9.___

    A. person who holds the typed copy is called the reader
    B. two members of a proofreading team should take turns in reading the typed copy aloud
    C. typed copy should be checked by the person who did the typing
    D. person who did not do the typing should read aloud from the typed copy

10. According to the above passage,

10.___

    A. it is unnecessary to read the period at the end of a sentence
    B. typographical errors should be noted on the original copy
    C. each person should develop his own set of proofreading marks
    D. figures should be read twice

Questions 11-16.

DIRECTIONS: Questions 11 through 16 are to be answered SOLELY on the basis of the above passage.

Basic to every office is the need for proper lighting. Inadequate lighting is a familiar cause of fatigue and serves to create a somewhat dismal atmosphere in the office. One requirement of proper lighting is that it be of an appropriate intensity. Intensity is measured in foot candles. According to the Illuminating Engineering Society of New York, for casual seeing tasks such as in reception rooms, inactive file rooms, and other service areas, it is recommended that the amount of light be 30 foot-candles. For ordinary seeing tasks such as reading, work in active file rooms, and in mailrooms, the recommended lighting is 100 foot-candles. For very difficult seeing tasks such as accounting, transcribing, and business machine use, the recommended lighting is 150 foot-candles.

Lighting intensity is only one requirement. Shadows and glare are to be avoided. For example, the larger the proportion of a ceiling filled with lighting units, the more glare-free and comfortable the lighting will be. Natural lighting from windows is not too dependable because on dark wintry days, windows yield little usable light, and on sunny summer afternoons, the glare from windows may be very distracting. Desks should not face the windows. Finally, the main lighting source ought to be overhead and to the left of the user,

11. According to the above passage, insufficient light in the office may cause

    A. glare   B. tiredness
    C. shadows   D. distraction

11.____

12. Based on the above passage, which of the following must be considered when planning lighting arrangements? The

    A. amount of natural light present
    B. amount of work to be done
    C. level of difficulty of work to be done
    D. type of activity to be carried out

12.____

13. It can be inferred from the above passage that a well-coordinated lighting scheme is LIKELY to result in

    A. greater employee productivity
    B. elimination of light reflection
    C. lower lighting cost
    D. more use of natural light

13.____

14. Of the following, the BEST title for the above passage is

    A. CHARACTERISTICS OF LIGHT
    B. LIGHT MEASUREMENT DEVICES
    C. FACTORS TO CONSIDER WHEN PLANNING LIGHTING SYSTEMS
    D. COMFORT VS. COST WHEN DEVISING LIGHTING ARRANGEMENTS

14.____

15. According to the above passage, a foot-candle is a measurement of the

    A. number of bulbs used
    B. strength of the light
    C. contrast between glare and shadow
    D. proportion of the ceiling filled with lighting units

15.____

16. According to the above passage, the number of foot-candles of light that would be needed to copy figures onto a payroll is _____ foot-candles.

    A. less than 30   B. 100
    C. 30   D. 150

16.____

Questions 17-23.

DIRECTIONS: Questions 17 through 23 are to be answered SOLELY on the basis of the following passage, which is the Fee Schedule of a hypothetical college.

FEE SCHEDULE

A. A candidate for any baccalaureate degree is not required to pay tuition fees for undergraduate courses until he exceeds 128 credits, Candidates exceeding 128 credits in undergraduate courses are charged at the rate of $100 a credit for each credit of undergraduate course work in excess of 128. Candidates for a baccalaureate degree who are taking graduate courses must pay the same fee as any other student taking graduate courses

B. Non-degree students and college graduates are charged tuition fees for courses, whether undergraduate or graduate, at the rate of $180 a credit. For such students, there is an additional charge of $150 for each class hour per week in excess of the number of course credits. For example, if a three-credit course meets five hours a week, there is an additional charge for the extra two hours. Graduate courses are shown with a (G) before the course number.

C. All students are required to pay the laboratory fees indicated after the number of credits given for that course.

D. All students must pay a $250 general fee each semester.

E. Candidates for a baccalaureate degree are charged a $150 medical insurance fee for each semester. All other students are charged a $100 medical insurance fee each semester.

17. Miss Burton is not a candidate for a degree. She registers for the following courses in the spring semester: Economics 12, 4 hours a week, 3 credits; History (G) 23, 4 hours a week, 3 credits; English 1, 2 hours a week, 2 credits. The TOTAL amount in fees that Miss Burton must pay is   17.__

    A. less than $2000
    B. at least $2000 but less than $2100
    C. at least $2100 but less than $2200
    D. $2200 or over

18. Miss Gray is not a candidate for a degree. She registers for the following courses in the fall semester: History 3, 3 hours a week, 3 credits; English 5, 3 hours a week, 2 credits; Physics 5, 6 hours a week, 3 credits, laboratory fee $ 60; Mathematics 7, 4 hours a week, 3 credits. The TOTAL amount in fees that Miss Gray must pay is   18.__

    A. less than $3150
    B. at least $3150 but less than $3250
    C. at least $3250 but less than $3350
    D. $3350 or over

19. Mr. Wall is a candidate for the Bachelor of Arts degree and has completed 126 credits. He registers for the following courses in the spring semester, his final semester at college: French 4, 3 hours a week, 3 credits; Physics (G) 15, 6 hours a week, 3 credits, laboratory fee $80; History (G) 33, 4 hours a week, 3 credits. The TOTAL amount in fees that this candidate must pay is   19.__

    A. less than $2100
    B. at least $2100 but less than $2300
    C. at least $2300 but less than $2500
    D. $2500

20. Mr. Tindall, a candidate for the B.A. degree, has completed 122 credits of undergraduate courses. He registers for the following courses in his final semester: English 31, 3 hours a week, 3 credits; Philosophy 12, 4 hours a week, 4 credits; Anthropology 15, 3 hours a week, 3 credits; Economics (G) 68, 3 hours a week, 3 credits. The TOTAL amount in fees that Mr. Tindall must pay in his final semester is   20.__

    A. less than $1200
    B. at least $1200 but less than $1400
    C. at least $1400 but less than $1600
    D. $1600

21. Mr. Cantrell, who was graduated from the college a year ago, registers for graduate courses in the fall semester. Each course for which he registers carries the same number of credits as the number of hours a week it meets.
If he pays a total of $1530; including a $100 laboratory fee, the number of credits for which he is registered is

    A. 4   B. 5   C. 6   D. 7

           21.____

22. Miss Jayson, who is not a candidate for a degree, has, registered for several courses including a lecture course in History. She withdraws from the course in History for which she had paid the required course fee of $690. The number of hours that this course is scheduled to meet is

    A. 4   B. 5   C. 2   D. 3

           22.____

23. Mr. Van Arsdale, a graduate of a college is Iowa, registers for the following courses in one semester: Chemistry 35, 5 hours a week, 3 credits; Biology 13, 4 hours a week, 3 credits, laboratory fee $150; Mathematics (G) 179, 3 hours a week, 3 credits.
The TOTAL amount in fees that Mr. Van Arsdale must pay is

           23.____

    A. less than $2400
    B. at least $2400 but less than $2500
    C. at least $2500 but less than $2600
    D. at least $2600 or over

Questions 24-25.

DIRECTIONS: Questions 24 and 25 are to be answered SOLELY on the basis of the following passage.

A duplex envelope is an envelope composed of two sections securely fastened together so that they become one mailing piece. This type of envelope makes it possible for a first class letter to be delivered simultaneously with third or fourth class matter and yet not require payment of the much higher first class postage rate on the entire mailing. First class postage is paid only on the letter which goes in the small compartment, third or fourth class postage being paid on the contents of the larger compartment. The larger compartment generally has an ungummed flap or clasp for sealing. The first class or smaller compartment has a gummed flap for sealing. Postal regulations require that the exact amount of postage applicable to each compartment be separately attached to it.

24. On the basis of the above passage, it is MOST accurate to state that

           24.____

    A. the smaller compartment is placed inside the larger compartment before mailing
    B. the two compartments may be detached and mailed separately
    C. two classes of mailing matter may be mailed as a unit at two different postage rates
    D. the more expensive postage rate is paid on the matter in the larger compartment

25. When a duplex envelope is used, the

    A. first class compartment may be sealed with a clasp
    B. correct amount of postage must be placed on each compartment
    C. compartment containing third or fourth class mail requires a gummed flap for sealing
    D. full amount of postage for both compartments may be placed on the larger compartment

———

KEY (CORRECT ANSWERS)

1. A		11. C	
2. D		12. D	
3. B		13. A	
4. B		14. C	
5. C		15. B	
6. A		16. D	
7. C		17. B	
8. B		18. A	
9. C		19. B	
10. D		20. B	

21. C
22. A
23. C
24. C
25. B

———

10/20
1

CPSIA information can be obtained
at www.ICGtesting.com
Printed in the USA
LVHW060638150719
624058LV00012B/120/P